First Time Press Release Number: 5
Frist Time Press 2021 Catalog Release Number: 1
Orginal Release Date: 02/01/2021

Published by First Time Press
a protected series of S.C. TreeHouse, LLC
3928 Pattentown Rd. Ooltewah, USA, TN 37363
www.firsttimepress.sctreehouse.com

Printed in the United States of America

Bad Father Good Father
Copyright © 2019 by Laura Schonlau
www.storytellers.systems

Cover design: Storytellers

All rights reserved. This book or any portion thereof may not be reproduced or transmitted in any manner, electronic, mechanical, including recording and photocopying whatsoever without the express written permission of the publisher.

Published in association with Storytellers, a protected series of S.C. TreeHouse, LLC, and S.C. TreeHouse Press, a protected series of S.C. TreeHouse, LLC, and Laura Schonlau.

FIRST TIME PRESS and First Time Press' logo are registered trademarks of S.C. TreeHouse, LLC.

Printed in the United States of America.
ISBN: 978-1-7366172-0-5

Edited by Laura Schonlau
Designed by Christopher D. Stewart

ISBN 978-1-7366172-0-5

bad father
Good Father

by
LAURA SCHONLAU

Stories from
Three Abused Women's Saving Grace

First Time Press
A Storytellers Company

WELCOME

First Time
Press

Welcome

Thank you for choosing to read this First Time Press book. As First Time Press we exist to give promising authors a platform to publish their early works. Since our founding, First Time Press has eagerly sought out and received submissions from authors worldwide looking for a chance to be noticed for their extraordinary creations.

What you are about to experience is raw talent. The following book has not been altered or edited by us (the publisher); instead, it is left exactly as the author wrote it. This is a showcase of an unaltered creation that we hope can inspire you to take a risk and let yourself and your work be seen.

We appreciate you taking the time to read this work of art and invite you to share in worshipping the God who has taught us all how to create.

Without further ado, we are proud to present to you the book, Bad Father Good Father, and we are honored to welcome Laua Schonlau to First Time Press.

Sincerely,
Christopher D. Stewart
Founder and Owner

Just as a father has compassion on his children, so the Lord has compassion on those who fear Him.

- Psalm 103:13

Contents

Introduction: 2

PART I
Bianca: 6
Sybil: 16
Chastain: 26

PART II
Bianca: 38
Sybil: 48
Chastain: 58

PART III
Bianca: 68
Sybil: 78
Chastain: 88

PART IV
Bianca: 102
Sybil: 114
Chastain: 124

PART V
Bianca: 136
Sybil: 146
Chastain: 158

PART VI
Bianca: 170
Sybil: 184
Chastain: 196

PART VII
Bianca: 206
Sybil: 220
Chastain: 230
Epilogue: 238

APPENDIX
Meet Laura Schonlau: ix
About First Time Press: xi
Titles From First Time: xiii

INTRODUCTION

Introduction

Walking home after a late night at work seems like just the thing she needs. Tax season completely drains her and she loves the cool night air. Stopping off for a cup of coffee to ward off the chill of the night, she just needs to clear her mind of numbers and clients. Working as a CPA is very rewarding, even during the stress of this season. Busy streets in the distance remind her another long day has been wrapped up, and the end of tax season is near. This makes her feel light and airy, knowing there's an end to the chaos.

As she nears her apartment, the thought of a long hot bath with a glass of wine sounds fabulous. Being lost in her own thoughts she doesn't pay much attention to her surroundings. That bath is sounding better and better the closer to home she gets. The dark shadows of the night engulfing her and would leave plenty of room for her thoughts to run wild if she allowed them to go there.

Stepping up to the porch of her apartment, she fumbles for keys in her purse. She shut the alarm off but the darn porch light is out, leaving little visibility to find her keys. Finally, there they are. Buried into a deep pocket on the inside of her purse. She lets out a sigh of relief as she begins to unlock the door. Then she hears the footsteps that are coming near to her. Trying to hurry to get in, as a leery feeling takes over the pit of her stomach, he says her name. She looks back but he has a dark hoody on and she is frightened as she steps through the door. Before she can get it locked back, the figure shoves his way into her apartment. He has a large knife pointing at her. He threatens to gut her like a fish if she makes a sound. Then he lunges toward her, knocking her to the ground. In a flash he had a piece of duct tape over her mouth and began dragging her to the bedroom. As she's struggling to get out of his grip, the candle sticks on the coffee table tumble over, the small table in the hallway gets knocked onto its side, the knife cuts her forearm and he throws her onto the bed. Stricken with fear she doesn't know what to do or how to protect herself in this position. Visions of her childhood begin flashing through her mind and she knows, deep inside, no man will ever take advantage of her again. As he comes toward her and lifts the hem of her skirt, he tells her "once I told you one day I would own you but you thought you had escaped". She begins to come to her senses. He's overpowering her when

Introduction

suddenly she grabs the ice pick she keeps under the pillow for protection in case anyone ever did get this close to her. Without a moments hesitation she stabs him in the neck. A deep animal groan came from him. She shoved him and he rolled over on the bed. She jumped up realizing she still had the tape over mouth and ripped it off. There was a pool of blood forming on her bed from the man. She ran for her purse to get her cell phone to call 911.

When the police arrived, she was ushered out of the apartment. Her neighbors had come out to see what was going on and that was then reality sunk in and she began to sob. What was a horrible situation just got worse when she found out who her attacker was.

PART I
BIANCA

PART I - Bianca

Bianca was such a sassy little girl. Dark, thick red hair her mother kept cut short. Bianca was such a tomboy and took no time to mess with her hair. Her mother kept it cut in a short bob so that it wasn't always a disheveled mess. You could get lost in her wide set blue eyes. She had a ruddy complexion and was very sarcastic. She was of average build but with short legs. She sported a broad forehead and thin lips. Her mother always tried to keep her nails cut short or Bianca would run around with broken, chipped, and dirty nails without any thought. Bianca has a hight pitched voice that can pierce the night when she raises her it.

Bianca has a younger sister, Dana. Dana is 8 years younger and adores everything about Bianca.

Her family lived in Freemont, Nebraska. Her father, Damien, was an assistant manager at a large local company which was most popular for Spam. It wasn't a big town. During the early 80's it was a town of approximately 23,000 people. Her mother, Annette, worked part time as a substitute teacher. Their basic needs were always met. Bianca loved when they would go on road trips. Her favorite was to travel anywhere that she could climb trees, play in the dirt or just roughhouse in general. Her childhood was one of unbridled passion and fun.

Her father had a sister, Demi and her mother had two sisters, Anna and Amy with 1 brother Aaron.

Her idea of having fun was playing football or basketball with the boys. On the playground at school, she always had to try to be better than the boys. If they were crossing the monkey bars, she had to catch up to and preferably pass them. As one young man was crossing she had a hard time catching up so when she got to where he was she put her hand over his and applied her weight as pressure to make him let go so she could beat him. She loved sports. Running track, high jump, and broad jump were her favorites. Competing in grade school at the end of the year was a highlight for her. She always won in each competition.

In fourth grade she had a teacher she absolutely adored. They got to do a lot of outside activities and even hatched duck and chicken eggs in the classroom. Mrs. Holmes will never know the lasting impact she had on Bianca.

Her parents were well known and they went to various activities and events. Her mother, Annette, love to attend catered parties. It made

PART I - Bianca

her feel pampered. During catered parties, many times Bianca was left to take care of her baby sister, Dana. Although Bianca was young, she was very responsible. Dana was a toddler with an early bedtime making taking care of her quite easy.

It was at a catered event her mother met a man named Milo. He was very attentive to Annette although he was not really supposed to mingle with the guests, he was quite smitten with Annette and visited her table repeatedly.

At a company picnic, Annette bumped into Milo again. He was helping clean up. They introduced themselves and she told him she remembered him as her server that did not give her time to ask for anything but was always right there with the next thing she might possibly need. It was if he could read her mind. He was relieved she remembered him and gave her his phone number in case she ever had a party or anything so he could be of assistance. Bianca came bounding up with Dana on her hip. Smiling broadly, she said hi to the man then asked her mom who he was. Bianca had come to find her mom because Dana needed a change of clothes and Bianca couldn't find anything. Milo complimented Dana on being such a great big sister and obviously a huge help to her mom. Annette excused herself and the girls, all waving goodbye to Milo.

Her family was a pretty average upper middle class family. Her dad was gone a lot with work. Annette took care of the girls and attended Bianca's track meets and school functions.

While Bianca was playing at the park, she saw Milo there one day. He was sitting by himself on a bench. She went over and said hello, asking if he had kids there, which he did not. She asked if he was married, which he was not. She asked why he came to the park if he was not going to play. Milo explained that sometimes he just enjoys sitting at the park, watching the kids play and listening to their laughter. She went on her way. Bianca told her mom that she had seen Milo at the park and Annette exclaimed that she would have to take Dana to the park also next time Bianca went.

The following week, Annette and the girls went to the park. After a bit, Milo arrived. Annette went over to talk with him while the girls were playing. They made small talk and laughed at some of Bianca's antics. She could be very theatrical in her performances. Milo mentioned how much he admired her. This

PART I - Bianca

made Annette very proud.

As Annette left with the girls, Milo watched her. She kept her hair up. He wondered how long it really was and what she would look like if it were down. As they walked away, he noticed Bianca actually had the same sashay to her walk that her mother did. That surprised him a bit considering what a tomboy Bianca was.

Fall soon arrived. Annette had only seen Milo once other than when they met at the park. It was always such a nice visit. She wished Damien would make the time to sit and listen to her. He was so busy. She missed him but couldn't change the circumstances. He was who he was and loved his job. He took very good care of her and the girls. So why did she feel so alone and even rejected. After the incident at the park she doubted she would ever see Milo again. She had been there with the girls and lost track of time during her chatter to Milo. Damien showed up demanding she get home and get the girls cleaned up and supper on the table. After arriving home, Damien did ask about Milo and how they knew each other. She shrugged it off loosely saying he was just another parent at the park she visited with that day to ward off her boredom. Damien didn't like it. He told her as much. He felt something off about the guy that did not settle with him well. He commented that Milo was probably a loser with nothing better to do. To Annette's surprise this made her angry. Bianca overheard the conversation and told her father that Milo was not a loser, he was a very nice man. Damien had no idea how much his wife had began talking to Milo on the phone.

The Fall Fair soon arrived. It was unusually cold, but the whole family ventured out to have some fun. As Bianca was riding the Octopus, Damien spotted Milo. He turned to his wife and said, well, your loser even made it out. Again this infuriated Annette. When Bianca finished the ride, Annette took her and Dana to the bathroom. Milo had been keeping an eye on her and moved toward the bathroom exits. He was elated to get to talk to Annette in person if only for a few minutes.

Annette began going to meet Milo. Usually at the mall so it looked like they accidentally bumped into one another. They would sit in the Food Court and talk over coffee. Milo chided Annette about having a husband who was not really a husband at all. He was rarely home at decent hours, was gone a lot and did not seem to express affection to Annette in public. Annette

PART I - BIANCA

did not stand up for Damien or make excuses. She found it very invigorating that Milo had taken such notice. Milo was so understanding, always willing to be there and just did not seem to be able to get enough of Annette. Annette's love for her husband was waining as she became more and more attached to Milo. She always wanted to spend more time with him. By now, her husband working late hours or not being home did not phase her much. She had Milo to rely on.

By Christmas, Annette was ready to leave her husband for Milo. She knew she could not do it during the holidays but she had begun stashing away money so she could leave soon thereafter. She wanted and desired this man that made her feel beautiful, important, loved, and cared for. Milo had helped her to see what a miserable marriage she had.

In mid-January, Annette moved out. Damien came home to a note on the kitchen counter. Annette told him to get a maid, she would serve the same purpose as Annette had for years. She expressed her disdain and let him know she was never coming back. Damien was broken hearted. He really did love Annette. He was just trying to be a great provider and take care of her and the kids. He wondered how he had missed her being so unhappy. His sadness turned to anger as he thought of all he did for his family. Then Annette has the audacity to take the girls and just move out? Surely, she had taken leave of her senses. On one hand he wanted her back home. On the other hand, what was the use? Why continue in what she explained as a loveless marriage where she no longer had any feelings, other than contempt, for him. Bianca had not wanted to leave her school and friends. Dana was too young to know the difference. Bianca already missed her dad and did not understand why they had to move without him. She was now in the 5th grade and this felt like the worst thing in the world to her. She just wanted her dad.

PART I - Bianca

PART I
SYBIL

PART I - Sybil

Sybil - a striking girl with fine, raven black, medium length hair. The color of her hair, her smooth skin with olive complexion made her green eyes very striking. Full lips with an oval shape face and high hairline made her very distinguishable among other children. She carries herself well and has a soft soothing voice. She has a very generous and loving nature.

She lived in Charleston, West Virginia with her father, James, her mother, Athena and 2 older brothers, William & Mason. With her beautiful silky hair the humidity in the summers didn't affect her. Charleston was not a metropolitan area but was a decent size town of about 71,000 people.

Her loving, kind nature automatically drew people to her. She was a girly girl that loved to dress up and play with makeup. She was also rather shy.

Her father worked for the city. He had 1 brother, Jacob. Her mother, Athena, was an office manager for a local Dr.'s office. Athena had 2 brothers, Logan & Sebastian and 1 sister Davina. They were a standard hardworking middle class family.

Sybil had 2 older brothers, William and Mason. She looked up to them and always wanted to go anywhere they were going. Many times her little heart got broken because she was not old enough to go with them. Their mom was not sure they would actually keep an eye on her. She was every bit the baby of the family and spoiled.

Every year they would go on vacation and visit grandparents in Georgia. It was always an exciting time of the year. The shells, warm waters, beaches and hours of fun in the sun. It was very humid there and made Sybil's hair rather unmanageable at times, so pigtails it was the majority of the time.

Sybil did her best to mind at home. She had seen her father get mad at her brothers and hit them or leave bruises on them with a belt. She always cried when it happened but could do nothing to stop it. If she pleaded with her dad to stop he would ask her if she wanted some of it and she would run to her mom. Those times were very scary for her. She loved her father and was scared of him at the same time. It wasn't that the boys were bad boys, they just made irresponsible stupid decisions according to her dad so they had to learn their lessons the hard way. Sybil was only a second grader and both of her brothers were in Jr. High. Back then Jr. High

PART I - Sybil

was 7th-9th grade. William was in ninth grade and Mason in seventh grade.

They were a church going family and Sybil loved Vacation Bible School in the summer. Another big day in the summer was the 4th of July. They loved going to the Riverfront for a cookout and the fireworks display to follow. On the way home James was extremely mad at William. He had been caught kissing a girl at the fireworks show. James said he refused to have illegitimate grandchildren that he would have to raise. William was trying to tell him it was nothing like that. It was the first time he had ever kissed her and she had been his girlfriend since May. His father would tell him to shut up if he could not tell the truth. He said he was young once and knew exactly what was going on. He went on to say it was exactly how he got stuck having to marry Athena. William was grounded to home until James said different. What a great way this was to start his Sophomore year.

As the kids were getting ready for school break for Christmas holidays, Sybil brought home a report card that had a U on one of her subjects. Her mother discussed it with her and she thought that was the end of it. Then her dad got home and saw it. He yelled for Sybil to come to him. He demanded to know why the bad grade. When she said she really did not know, he became furious asking her if she did not know, who did? Her mom told him they had talked about it and everything would be ok. Sybil began to cry. Her fathered yelled are you kidding me? Now you're going to cry? That is what gets you out of everything, is that what you think? How about I just ground you through the whole holiday and no presents for Christmas? How would you like that? Sybil shook her head no. James told her to speak up, a nod was not an answer. Her mother asked if it was necessary to be this hard on her. Big mistake. James took 2 steps toward Athena and backhanded her in the mouth. Blood trickled at the corner of her mouth and her top lip immediately began to swell. He looked at Sybil and asked if she needed some of that too? There was no nod of the head this time, instead she answered no, sir. He told her to go to bed without supper for her punishment and that he better never see that grade on her report card again. She went to her room and cried herself to sleep.

Frequently, Sybil's father would go to the local bar and stay out late. Sometimes he came home and went to bed. Other times he would be

PART I - Sybil

loud and yelling, waking everyone up. Athena hated this behavior but had learned much earlier in the marriage that saying anything or becoming argumentative with him had harsh physical results. She would just leave him be until he passed out and then wake him for work the next morning.

Sybil's father always seemed to be in an uproar about something. If it was not his wife or one of the kids, it was the neighbors. They were too loud, not sociable enough, didn't mow their grass often enough…there was always something for him to complain about with each neighbor. Everything was always someone else's fault. Due to his 'terrible' surroundings (which included the kids and wife) he would say, 'if it wasn't for bad luck, he'd have no luck at all.'

As time passed James' temper seemed to increase. One of the boys was always doing something wrong and getting a beating for it. He belittled them at every turn making sure they knew they would never amount to anything and would never be enough for anything they wanted to do. It was so hard on Sybil. She loved her brothers and didn't want to see the things that happened to them but couldn't possibly always avoid it. She tried. At all cost she tried not to cause trouble or do anything that would set off her daddy's temper. She was scared and crying most of the time. She just wanted it all to stop and for everyone to like each other. She longed to hear the words 'I love you' rather than 'are you that stupid'. Her friends did not talk of their daddies acting the way hers did. She wondered if that meant their daddies didn't love them as much as hers did. He only wanted his kids to do right, grow up and be somebody and not get into any kind of trouble. It was confusing for Sybil at best. Maybe it did happen at her friends house but their daddies also told them they better not tell. That was what she decided she would believe. Things happen at home that are not to be repeated outside of it.

There were times her brothers and dad would wrestle. Her dad got very mad if one of the boys would happen to pin him. Afterwards, he was hateful and grumpy at best. He would always tell them not to let their britches get too big, everyone got lucky now and then. One day he decided to wrestle with Sybil. He was a bit rough and it made her cry. He made her get back in the living room and told her to suck it up. This time during the wrestling Sybil really didn't like it because of the places he would put

PART I - Sybil

his hands. At school they taught you to tell if someone touched you in bad places. When she began to fuss about it, her dad said no one was ever any fun in this house. Her mother consoled her and told her what she learned at school was right but it did not apply to daddies. A daddy would never do things to his daughter that were not approved of. Her mother encouraged her to go back to the living room and tell her daddy she was sorry for the way she acted and to give him a big hug. For the time being, there was peace.

Sybil loved to have her nails painted so her mother did her fingers and toes the next day. It made Sybil feel grown up, other than the fact her mom wouldn't let her do it herself yet. Still, she loved the pretty color and could not wait to show her friends.

In William's Senior Year, things were hectic and James complained continually about the extra money being spent! It was everyday drama to hear about it. Then William brought his girlfriend over around Valentine's Day. They wanted to talk to mom and dad, alone. They had asked Mason and I to go to our rooms. A lot of good that did. You could probably hear my dad yelling at the other end of the block. William and his girlfriend were expecting a baby. Sybil's dad was enraged at the news. He was yelling at them and telling them how they have ruined their lives and the lives of both families since they would probably have to pay for everything. William had a plan to go into the Marines after graduation. His dad had already told him that he would never make it. Now he was telling him, he had no chance at all. Everyone was in tears. William had hoped it would not go this way but in the back of his mind knew exactly what to expect. His girlfriend was sobbing and all he wanted to do was comfort her. He explained they had already planned to marry after High School anyway, and that this just moves things up a little faster. His dad was seething and told him not to bother graduating now because he always knew William would never be worth anything and this just proved it. Athena was trying to get James to calm down to no avail. If anything it seemed to make him more mad. He told William to get out. Since he thought he was all grown up, just get out and there will be no graduation because he was not wasting another dime on him. William and his girlfriend left. Athena actually raised her voice to James regarding the way he acted. She did not want William kicked out of the house. She wanted to

PART I - SYBIL

see him graduate and get married. It wasn't the perfect situation but it was their grandchild.

William came by to get some clothes. His girlfriends parents had allowed him to stay with them. Athena told him that he could come home but he refused telling her not until he heard his dad say it. He gave her a big hug, whispered 'I'm sorry' and left. His mother began to cry. She had never understood her husband's temper but now he had gone as far to kick their son out. She and James had made the exact same mistake. She did not understand why he saw it as the end of the world, it had worked out for them and it could for William as well.

William and Gayla planned a small wedding. They were very much in love with one another and wanted to go ahead with the plans they had already had. William would go into the military but now Gayla would be a wife and mom instead of just a wife. Her parents helped them out and they got an apartment. William graduated and his mother, brother and sister were there for it. Then he went from part-time to full-time at his job. The plan was to wait for the baby to be born.

PART I
CHASTAIN

PART I - Chastain

Chastain was a beautiful little girl with long blonde, naturally wavy hair with a heart shaped face. She had big deep set dark brown eyes that reminded you of a doe. With a fair complexion she always had to be careful in the sun. She was of a petite build with cupid bow lips. She had the heart shaped face which accented her lips and eyes. She was always one of the shorter girls. Short, petite fingers which she continuously bit to the quick. She sported a thick waistline with a happy, carefree attitude. Her voice was throaty, almost raspy sounding. She had a happy but focused personality.

She grew up with her parents in the Upper Class NE Quadrant of Albuqerque, New Mexico. with approximately 250,000 people. Her father, Robert, was a real estate mogul and her mother, Donna, stayed at home taking care of her every need. Donna never missed a class project, musical, awards assembly, recital, etc. Chastain was very loved and taken care of. She had the best of everything. Her mother saw to that. Her father simply adored her and she was definitely daddy's little girl.

But there were secrets. Her father was gone most of the time. She thought her parents were happy but their marriage was rocky at best.

Her father had a twin brother, Rhett, and her mother had 2 sisters, Dahlia and Daphne . Chastain was an only child due to complications for her mother at birth. The family were all very close and she saw her relatives often. Life seemed so good then.

Her father and grandfather played chess and she was fascinated by the game. The chessboard held so many surprises and she was beginning to learn to play. Her father always encouraged her that as she got older she could be on the Chess Team. To Chastain, that was the most wonderful thing she had ever heard. Her dad and grandpa could teach her how to play and she would be at an advantage against her opponents once she became a member of the Chess Club.

Her Uncle Rhett lived with them off and on. Her mother said he was a bum and just wanted to live off them and not have to work. Her father saw it differently. He never wanted Rhett to feel as though no one loved or cared about him when he was down on his luck. Yes, Robert knew Rhett had lived with them too many times but it was his little brother and he couldn't turn him away. Rhett wasn't much of a chess player. He actually found the game repulsive, which was hard for Chastain to understand. She loved

PART I - Chastain

the game and the challenges it brought.

Chastain's academics came naturally. Her friends were in awe of her grades and how little she had to study. Other girls at school were hateful and hurtful with their words to Chastain. They referred to her as 'little miss perfect'. Her father told her they were just jealous but, it still hurt. She had never done anything to those girls, so why were they being mean to her?

Her mother encouraged her to ignore them and focus on her friends that love her. She kept Chastain's hope up by promising to send her to Finishing School. Chastain loved to dress up and the thought of learning to be a lady and social graces were thrilling to her. She couldn't wait for it. She would get to do that before she joined the Chess Team. She felt as though she were already becoming refined at just the mere thought of it.

Her father's work in real estate made it so he was gone a lot in the evenings and on weekends. Her mother would record her recitals and awards assembly's so the three of them could watch together when her dad had more time. Those times were cherished by Chastain. Her parents had no idea how much those special moments meant to her.

There were times her father had to go out of town for a few days for meetings, conferences, etc. It seemed to Chastain that he was being gone more. Maybe it just felt that way because her friends parents were both home more often than hers. Sometimes she would daydream about what it would be like to have both of her parents home every evening and all the things they would do together. She had a very active imagination that could carry her away for long periods of time. Then she would settle down and realize the truth was she would not really know what to do if life was really that way. This life was what she was happy and familiar with.

The school year had come to an end. In a way, Chastain was relieved. Her body had begun to change and she found it embarrassing. The hair on her legs had begun to become fuller and darker and it was showing up in her armpits as well! She went to her mother in tears. She explained these changes that were happening and felt something was wrong with her. Her mother consoled her and said some of the other girls may have already started shaving and she would teach her how. This made Chastain feel a little better but she was rather anxious about having a razor on her legs and armpits. Once

PART I - Chastain

she had shaved she felt so much better and was no longer so self-conscious about what she thought was making her weird and different. She was still completely aware of other changes happening but her mother had confirmed they were all normal and all girls go through this. She was feeling better about starting sixth grade.

The summer seemed to fly by. Chastain and her mother went to a few events at the Country Club, to the Ballet twice, a spa day once a month, several girls days out as well as time with her friends. The next thing she knew, school was about to start. Entering the sixth grade was exciting for her. It brought her 1 step closer to Finishing School and the Chess Team.

Her friends came over all excited and wanted her to try out for a spot as a cheerleader. They were hopeful the four of them would be picked and talked of the fun trips they would get to go on. Her mother said she should try out. So, the cheer practices began.

The second week of school, tryouts began. All four of the girls gave it their best and then had to wait for it to be posted on the billboard. The anticipation was killing them! Sure enough, all four had made it. Chastain's mother threw a little celebration party for them. Donna knew the girls loved to set up a table, pretend they were from England and have tea and crumpets. They didn't care if the 'crumpets' were pound cake, english muffins or cookies. They just loved to let their imaginations carry them away and pretend they were with the Queen. They would each dress up as though they were princesses. Their imaginations ran wild as they decided where in England they were today, sitting outside, enjoying their tea and crumpets while deciding what their environment looked like. So Donna made a very special table for them and let them have their fun with various crumpets.

Finally, the day had arrived! They each had received their cheerleading uniforms and pom-poms. Chastain hosted all the practices at their house. She had plenty of room and her mom always had refreshments for them.

One day after all the girls had left, she came in and heard her mom on the phone. She was talking quietly but you could tell she was upset. All Chastain heard was her mother say "you are telling me that you already have another conference to attend? I am not believing all the conferences any more, who is she?" Donna looked up and saw Chastain and immediately her scowl was gone and her voice changed. She

PART I - CHASTAIN

asked Chastain if she would like to talk to her father. Handing over the phone, Donna left the room trying not to cry in front of her daughter. Chastain was ecstatic to get to talk to her daddy and tell him all about the cheer squad.

After the conversation with her dad, she went to find her mom. She wanted to know what her mom was talking about and who this "she" was. Donna held Chastain in her arms and explained she was just upset that daddy was going to another 3 day conference. Chastain wasn't through with the conversation, she pressed on to know who the 'she' was that was with her daddy. Her mother calmly explained, there was no 'she' but in a moment of really missing daddy she let her imagination run wild and there was nothing for her to worry about.

Chastain was still distraught that her mother had been unhappy. She had never seen her like that before. She knew her dad had been gone more than usual but another woman? Chastain dismissed the thought, knowing her daddy would never do that. Why would he? Everything he loved and wanted was right here.

The thoughts were racing through Donna's mind. The truth was, she did believe her husband had found someone else. She thought about what she had done wrong, why she was not enough or was it because she could not have more children so he would never have the son he wanted. That night she lie in bed crying softly so Chastain would not hear her. What she really wanted was to have a bawling fit, scream, maybe even throw something. How? How could Robert do something like this to her? To their daughter? She was awake most of the night with her mind running wild.

The next day Chastain was surprised to see her mom in leggings, an oversize shirt and her hair in a ponytail. Normally she was either still in one of her beautiful negligee's preparing breakfast or already pristinely dressed for the day. Donna explained she just want a comfy day without all the makeup and dressing up. After all, it's Saturday, let's just kick back and relax. That afternoon the doorbell rang. It was the florist with a huge bouquet of assorted flowers from Robert with a card that said, 'I love You'.

Monday after school, Chastain noticed her mother being very absent minded and a bit flustered. Finally, Donna shared that Rhett was moving back in again. She tried not to show disdain for him in front of Chastain, but she had had it. Rhett never kept a job, was always down

PART I - CHASTAIN

on his luck and always ran to Robert to take care of him. It wasn't like he was young and learning lessons. They had far surpassed that phase.

When Robert returned home, he and Donna had a heated discussion about him being gone so much and Rhett moving back in. Again she was accusing him of having someone else as well. To top it off, Rhett began moving into the spare room. Not only was he moving in but needed Robert to pay for his storage building. Same old words, same old Rhett. He'll be looking for a job, he won't outstay his welcome, he'll be out in no time. All things they had heard before.

The next day was cheerleading practice. Donna made treats ahead of time. She and Robert were actually going out on a date! She could not remember the last time they had done this. Robert told her not to worry about Chastain because Rhett would be there. As practice went on, Chastain saw a shadow by the back window. At first she thought she imagined it but a bit later noticed it again. It was her Uncle Rhett watching the girls practice. She went in to tell him to come out and join them but he was no longer by the window. He had gone back to his room with the door closed which meant not to bother him. She wished he would have come outside instead of being bashful.

Later in the week as Robert was in the shower, his phone rang. Donna picked it up and a woman's voice was on the end wanting to know who answered his phone and to put him on the line. Donna hung up. Her worst fears had just come true. When Robert got out of the shower Donna was waiting like a volcano about to erupt. Robert eventually confessed to having met someone that made him feel alive again. She made him remember what it was to enjoy life again, never nagged him about being gone and her attention was solely on him. Through many tears of the heartbreak, they decided he should move out. He thought he needed time to clear his mind and decide what he truly wanted. So help her, Donna absolutely could not figure out how any of this had happened. And to make it worse, she was stuck with Rhett being there.

PART I - CHASTAIN

PART II
BIANCA

PART II - BIANCA

Moving out was hard on both girls. Annette was elated to see Milo any time she wanted and talk to him to her hearts content. Milo had wanted Annette to just move in with him but Annette felt it was best to live on her own until her divorce was over. She loved the idea of getting to spend every evening with Milo.

Bianca looked forward to getting to go see her dad and stay in her real house. The one she lived in with her mom was ok but she missed the familiarity, her room, and comfort of her dad's house. Although the house she lived in with her mom was ok, the yard was small and the house smelled dank and musty. The people were much different. They were nice but dressed and acted differently than the people in her old neighborhood. And the houses were very close together. The grass was even different, it was as much dirt as grass. She wanted the yard she was used to that had more grass than dirt. She missed all of it. And most of all, she missed her friends. She was making some new ones but it just was not the same. Her school was much different as well. There were many more kids in once class than she was accustomed to. She felt like she just blended in to a sea of faces.

Her dad would take her and Dana shopping,

to the water park. the zoo, amusement park as well as watch movies and make popcorn with them. Sometimes he could not come and pick them up. Bianca tried to act like it was okay and that she understood. But she did not. She would cry herself to sleep wishing she could see him. Dana would ask for daddy and cry at times which made Bianca sad as well. Why did they have to leave? Why couldn't they go back home? She did not know the answers but hoped they would move back to their real home soon.

Why they moved was very confusing. Her mom said it was because daddy did not love her anymore. Daddy said he never stopped loving mommy. Damien pleaded with Annette to go to counseling and try to work the marriage out. Annette wouldn't have any of it. She was disagreeable to anything he asked of her. What Damien and the kids didn't know was that when the kids would go to their dads, Annette would go stay with Milo.

Damien despised the fact she still even spoke to Milo. He had no idea how their relationship had blossomed and was a focal point for Annette.

Annette had enough money and filed for divorce in March. Incompatibility and

PART II - Bianca

unhappiness were the reasons she used in her filing. When Damien was served she felt a sense of accomplishment. It was even better to her because she had him served at work. She was finally getting a footing in the life she wanted to live - Her life with Milo. If all went well, she would be divorced soon and be able to move in with Milo around the first of the year. What a fabulous way to kick off the New Year!

Next fall Bianca would start the sixth grade. She was growing up and Dana was getting so big. The following year Annette would be able to put Dana in Kindergarten. She did not plan to work once she lived with Milo. She only wanted to take care of him. The kids too but her infatuation with Milo was over the top. Her old friends would occasionally see her with Milo and usually did not strike up a conversation. She got the impression they did not care much for him. Oh well, that was their loss. At times Bianca would want one or two of her old friends to stay the night but their parents always said no. Finally, her dad asked if the girls could have a sleepover at his house and they agreed. They even helped furnish snacks. Bianca was so happy it did not bother her a bit that Dana was a pest.

Months went by. The divorce was finalized.

The holidays had arrived. Annette had brought home a tree. It looked nothing like a Christmas tree to Bianca. It was silver! And small! It sat on a table in the corner. They hung lights and placed ornaments and a star on top. No matter how much Bianca stared at it, it did not seem like a Christmas tree.

    The girls got to go to their dads the week before Christmas. They were so surprised to get to the house and Aunt Demi was there! She excitedly shared their plans for the weekend. They were going to pick out a tree, put it up, decorate the tree and the house and have hot chocolate to keep warm during it all. Aunt Demi made the best hot chocolate and even put a candy cane in it. That evening they went to a tree lot and picked out the perfect tree. Once they got it home, trimmed and set up, everyone was exhausted. The next morning the girls woke up to reindeer pancakes with bacon for the antlers. There was a strawberry for the red nose. The girls were delighted. They spent the morning decorating the tree and living room. That afternoon, her dad put up lights outside while the girls made homemade cookies with Aunt Demi. They were jubilant about their creations as they iced them! Sunday was a day of sleeping

PART II - Bianca

in and relaxing for the day. Just spending time visiting, talking about life and just keeping their connections strong.

When they returned to their Mom's, she was acting differently. Packing up some 'old things', singing and dancing around. She asked the girls if they would like to go back to their dad's for New Year's Eve. They were very excited about this and immediately called their dad. They wanted to plan a New Year's Party with their friends. He agreed and the girls were ecstatic and Bianca began writing down plans.

Christmas was quite different this year. They had presents, food, and fun but it did not seem as happy as previous years. Both girls wished their dad was there. They still had not adjusted to him not being with them.

New Year's Eve arrived quickly. The girls actually got to go the day before so they could get snacks and items for their party. They decided they wanted it to be their New Year's Jubilation. They picked up balloons and streamers to decorate the kitchen and living room. When Bianca's friends arrived there was a lot of giggling and whispering. One of the girls had a boyfriend and this was big news! At midnight they drank their Sparkling Grape Juice in clear plastic champagne flutes. They felt so grown up.

    The next morning looked like they had quite the party. Balloons were all over the floor, some of the streamers had fallen down, tons of snacks were left over in the kitchen and the girls were all sleeping peacefully in their sleeping bags. Once everyone was awake they all pitched in and cleaned up. Bianca reluctantly said goodbye to her friends as they left one by one. A part of her dreaded going back to her other house. It had been so much harder to try and make friends there. There weren't many girls her own age in her immediate neighborhood.

    The next day Damien took the girls back to Annette. Annette seemed totally distracted and immediately loaded the girls in the car. As Damien drove back home, he had a bit of an empty feeling in the pit of his stomach. He missed the girls and Annette.

    Annette quickly pulled out of the drive and started down the road. The girls asked where they were going and were told it was a surprise! This excited the girls and they could not wait to see what the surprise was! In a few minutes, they pulled into the driveway at Milo's house. The girls didn't dislike Milo, they just wanted their dad. Bianca asked why they were there. Her

PART II - Bianca

mother turned to her and told her that while they were gone, she and Milo had packed up all their belongings and moved them into Milo's house. This was not the kind of surprise Bianca or Dana thought they would be getting. This was not a surprise, this was disappointment. Bianca wondered why her mom would move them in with Milo? Why not back to their dads? It was not that they dislike Milo, they just wanted their parents back together.

Milo was all smiles as he came outside to welcome them. They were polite but unhappy. He took them inside to show them around. They each had their own room. Milo told them, they could play anywhere in the house but not the basement. The basement was his space, not a play area. He adamantly emphasized they did not have any reason to go down there. So life began with another new set up.

The house was ok but seemed small. Bianca went to her room to unpack her things. She wanted to be left alone. She wanted to cry. She wanted to scream but knew that wouldn't help the situation. As she was unpacking, Milo came in. He told her not to be sad. They would have a great time and he had surprises in store for her. It was not actually a comfort for Bianca. He did not understand and neither did her mom. Milo reached over to an open bag she had started to unpack. He pulled out a pair of panties and told her they were really nice and handed her all of her personal items and underwear from the bag. What a weird way to help her. She didn't like it and didn't want him touching any of her things anymore.

PART II - Bianca

PART II
SYBIL

PART II - Sybil

Sybil's father decided church was a waste of their time. He was talking of how long they had been going and giving away money that could have gone on the kids. He had decided they would no longer be attending. Athena was mortified. She loved their church, the pastor and his family, her friends but most of all Jesus. She inquired if that meant she, Sybil and Mason could no longer go. He had turned and looked at her as if she had attempted to slap him. His eyes grew dark and angry. He snapped at her that they can go if they want but there was no more giving money to the church. His wife wondered what had happened to his beliefs. Or to what beliefs she had thought he had. He turned and stared at Athena…"what has giving to the church gotten us so far?" A son who knocked up his girlfriend and ruined his life, Mason can't keep from making stupid decisions and she (referring to Sybil) will probably get knocked up and ruin our lives too! What, exactly, has this Jesus done for this family? He told her he was done with it and that was the end of it.

Sybil was going into the fifth grade by this time. She was excited to meet her new teacher and see old friends. She was such a loving and generous child. She wanted to make something to give to her teacher on the first day so she started looking in magazines to come up with an idea.

When James was at work, Athena would leave work and would sneak over and see about William and Gayla. Gayla had the cutest little belly. They found out they were having a girl and Athena was thrilled. She wanted to make the baby her first baby quilt. William continued to work hard to provide for his family and was doing a great job. He genuinely loved Gayla and was excited about his daughter. Gayla had decorated their place and it felt so comfortable and homey. Athena was so proud of her son and the man he had become. The way he stepped up in a situation that other young men might have run from. His father ran at first then came around reluctantly and married her because of the pressure from both sides of the family and a few friends too. Of course, William and Gayla always asked about Sybil and Mason. Sometimes William would hang his head and ask how his father was. The truth was there was no change. He was still harsh and had now turned on the church. William asked his mother if she ever wanted more? More than someone who treated her in such a lowly fashion, spoke ill of her

PART II - Sybil

and was downright mean many times. Athena assured William he would never understand. She had gone straight from her mom and dad's house to a house with James. She did not know any different and she was okay with it. She told him that sometimes you have to live with the mistakes you make. Her situation hadn't been a good one. His father did not marry her because he loved her but because she got pregnant and over the years she had come to accept that. What would she do anyway? She had no skills to land a better job. Furthermore where would she go. The world was a scary place to her.

    To Sybil there did not seem to be as much yelling and hitting these days. Her dad drank more at home but if that made him feel good and kept everyone from fighting, she was good with that. She had found a picture of a sunflower made of burlap with yellow and green material. She was so excited. She wanted to put a magnet on the back so her teacher could keep it and hang it up. Her mother thought it was a lovely idea and after supper they went together to get the materials. Sybil was overjoyed and decided she would make one for her mom too that way she always had a bright flower just for her.

    One evening, Athena asked James if

she could go to a ladies event at the church and promised she would be back by nine pm. Although he was unenthusiastic about it, he said yes as long and she did not put anything in the offering plate because he knew they would pass it around. Athena felt bad for never giving anything anymore but at least she could still go. She changed clothes and set out a snack for Sybil. Mason was out with friends. It was unusual for just he and Sybil to be at home together.

 Sybil entered the living room later to see what her dad was watching on tv. She got up in the chair and had no idea what the movie was about, but things were blowing up and people were shooting at each other. She got up to go back to her room when her dad interrupted her thoughts and told her to come sit with him on the couch. He began poking her with his elbow and she politely told him that she didn't like that. He wanted to know what she had against him wrestling with her. She told him that one time when he did it, he touched her in bad places and she did not like it. He wanted to know what on earth she was talking about! So she shared about him putting his hands on her chest and at school they were taught that was the 'no zone' and to tell someone if anyone touched

PART II - Sybil

you there. Just like her mother, he explained it was okay for daddies to do it. They would never hurt their little girls. He had her stand up and stand in front of him. He stretched both hands out towards her and placed one on each side of her chest. It made her feel embarrassed. Then he asked her if that had hurt. She admitted it did not. So he placed his hand inside her thigh and asked if that hurt. Again she admitted it did not. He allowed that daddies do those things as lessons for when their daughters get older. He asked if she wanted to wind up pregnant without a husband and she vehemently said no without hesitation. Her dad told her that was good because he did not want her to have to get married like he and her mom had to and then William and Gayle had to. He shared they could have had a soulmate out there and missed out because of mistakes but he was not going to let that happen to her. When he asked if that sounded good she said it sounded fantastic! Then she went on her way to have her bedtime snack. It was so weird when she got ready for bed. She'd never felt like someone was watching her before so she hurried and changed into her pajamas. She thought maybe Mason had come home and walked down the hall and she did not realize it. She dismissed it, read her book and turned out the light.

When her mother arrived back home she peeked in on Sybil who was fast asleep. She asked James how their evening went. He told her it was okay. He had watched a movie and Sybil basically entertained herself for the evening.

The next day Sybil was excited to put the finishing touches on the 2 sunflowers she made for her mom and teacher. She just knew they going to love them. As she worked diligently to make sure everything was perfect she felt overjoyed and began to sing quietly to herself. Finally, the last piece was done. She had made a burlap sunflower with a green and white plaid stem and 2 green leaves. Of course she remembered to put the magnet on the back so they could hang them up. She whisked her prize work off to her room to let the glue finish drying. She did not want her mom to see them when she got off work. Her mom worked hard as an office manager at a Dr.'s office. Everyone there was really nice.

That night her dad came home pretty late. He woke Sybil and Mason up with his loud booming voice. Mom was fussing at him for coming home drunk and he asked if she wanted

PART II - Sybil

him to leave. Of course she did not, she just wanted him to tone it down. The kids had school tomorrow and both of them had to get up and go to work. Dad was being loud when he raised his voice to Athena and asked if this was what kind of treatment he was going to get because she got to go visit with her Jesus loving freaks. He accused her of thinking she was better than him and he was sick and tired of her treating him like he was stupid. He yelled, I AM NOT STUPID! Mom started talking soothingly and got him to lie down on the couch and she turned the television on for him and sat with him until he passed out.

    The following weekend they had a cookout with some of dad's friends from work. Dad was drinking his Budweiser and mom was drinking her Boone's Farm Strawberry wine. Mason went out with friends. A couple of the families had kids also. Some were too young for her to play with so she started talking to a boy and girl and asked if they wanted to play washers or lawn darts. They started out with washers. The boy was very whiney and always going to tell on his sister for something. His sister was 2 grades ahead of Sybil but was very nice. She apologized for her brother, saying her mom babies him too much and she needs to let him grow up instead of always letting him act like a baby. Sybil's dad came over to the girls and asked if they were having a good time. He asked the other girl if she wanted a beer. She laughed and said her parents would kill her. James told the girl that he thought she looked like a grown woman and could drink. They all laughed and James stood between the two of them draping his arms over each of their shoulders. He brushed Sybil's chest a couple times and that was when she realized it really was okay. If it was not he wouldn't have done it. It appeared he brushed the other girls chest too. She removed her dad's arm from her shoulder and told them she should go find her parents. He hugged Sybil one more time and brushed his beer bottle against her chest. She thought that was an accident and that bottle was cold. A little later James was getting loud and belligerent telling people to go on home. He helped Athena put up the tables and chairs but a couple neighbors had come out to see what he was being so loud about. Mom got him to go into the house and to find something to watch on television. He seemed to be mellowing as he sat there staring at it. He would occasionally bark for Athena to bring him

PART II - Sybil

another beer. Sybil wondered if he even knew what he was watching. It had a bunch a girls dancing on it and that wasn't the type of thing he usually watched. He told Athena to get in the living room and sit on the couch with him and informed Sybil she needed to go to bed. When Mason got home, mom was covering dad up on the couch where he had passed out again. Try as he might, Mason did not know why his mother put up with it much less as gracefully as she did. One thing he knew was he never wanted to be a husband like his dad was much less the type of dad he was. He thought his dad was a lush and was embarrassed for people to find out who his dad was. Sometimes he would act like he had been adopted just so people would not think they were blood related.

PART II
CHASTAIN

PART II - Chastain

Robert began looking for his own place. Donna was totally beside herself. She was constantly thinking about what she had done wrong to make her marriage end. He could say he needed to clear his head but, Donna knew it was so he could spend more time with the other woman!

After many discussions, Robert and Donna knew they had to sit Chastain down and tell her about the changes about to take place. Chastain felt blindsided. When had all of this happened? Why was it happening to her family? Was she part of the reason daddy was leaving? Did she do something to make him that unhappy? How could he do this to her and her mom?

Chastain was not accepting of the situation. She wanted to know where daddy was moving. When was he moving? Had he already found an apartment? Why hadn't anyone told her about this before now? Would she get to see him? So many questions swirling impulsively through her mind. She began to cry. It was like unleashing a levee. As her parents tried to console her, it was not helping. She finally jumped up and ran to her room. Throwing herself on her bed, crying uncontrollably, she needed to snuggle up with her large stuffed teddy bear and spill all of her emotions out to him. She felt as though her life had ended. Who was going to help her with Chess and getting into the Chess Club? Why, oh why did this have to happen?

Later her father came to the door. He wanted to hold her tight and assure her that none of this was her fault. He knew it was all him. He knew it seemed selfish. As he whispered reassurances to her and let her know they would still see each other often, his eyes welled with tears as well. He had not given forethought to how this would affect her.

When he left the room, he began packing. He was moving into a Condo. Rhett came through and offered to help. His timing was all wrong. Right now Robert just wanted to get his things and get out. His feelings of guilt overwhelming him but not enough to make him stay.

The following day Rhett saw Chastain in the kitchen. He went in to visit with her and hopefully cheer her up some. Her eyes were all red and swollen from all the crying she had done. At first she was unresponsive to his small talk. Finally, he told her anything she might need her dad for, she could come to him. This filled Chastain with fury! Who did Uncle Rhett think he was? He would not be a substitute

PART II - CHASTAIN

daddy for her. No one could do that. He realized in her state of distress she was lashing out. She was such a beautiful girl and he hated seeing her like this.

Donna barely came out of her room that day. She was very tearful and started believing she knew what depression really feels like. She had a gaping hole in her heart, her stomach was tied in multiple knots that hurt as well. She had no desire to get out of bed and refused to face the day. How could she? Her life had been destroyed in the answering of a phone call meant for her husband. Had Robert not told the other woman he was married? Whether he had or not made no difference now. The damage was done and Robert had left her. Although he was still going to take care of her and Chastain financially, was of little relief at the moment.

Robert moved into his new condo. Once he was there he felt a sense of relief. He had finally owned up to his infraction and was now on his own. Still technically married but more than exhilarated at the thought of the time he could now spend with Rain. It felt so good, being able to say her name out loud. No more hiding. It was time to give her a call and let his new life begin. He was giving this a trial run to be sure it would work out before he divorced his wife. He thought it was better to be safe than sorry. When Rain answered the phone he nearly shouted for joy and told her to get on over to the condo. He was proud he had made the move and would be enjoying life, adventure, and love!

Uncle Rhett kept attempting to be there for Donna and Chastain. It was making Donna furious. If he wanted to do something why not get a job and his own place. That would help tremendously. She knew he wouldn't though. He was on the gravy train again and would stay that way for a while.

Chastain cancelled the next two cheerleading practices. How could she go be happy and cheering with the way she felt? She was convinced she could figure out how to make her daddy come back home. She wanted to meet this woman named Rain. What kind of a name was that anyway? All Chastain knew was that Rain was younger than her mom, had dark hair and dark features. She was the total opposite of her mom's fair hair and complexion.

Uncle Rhett kept trying to encourage her to start her cheerleading practices back up. He said he missed all the excitement of the girls and their cheering. He convinced her it would

PART II - CHASTAIN

brighten up the days to get started again and give her mom purpose by fixing the snacks and being there for the girls. Chastain conceded that it would probably help things out a little bit. She scheduled the next practice at her house for the following Saturday. Uncle Rhett was right. She was feeling a little happier now.

Rain would set up swanky dinners for her and Robert to enjoy. And enjoy he did. They would drink a bit too much, get too loud and have a great time with friends. He could not remember the last time he and Donna had done such a thing. Donna would have wanted them all out had they behaved this way in her house. He chuckled to himself as he thought about the right decision he had made.

He loved to see Rain happy so he scheduled a vacation to Dubai. 10 days of pure bliss with the woman of his dreams. He knew this would make Donna mad so he just told her that he had a couple conferences to go to during that time. He wondered how he got so lucky to find Rain and have a shot at happiness in his life. She could be demanding, a bit uncontrollable at times, high maintenance but he loved her all the same.

Chastain continued having practices at

her house. It was so weird the way her Uncle would watch them from inside the house. It was starting to bother her but she wasn't sure why. She finally mentioned it to her mom. Her mother told her not to worry about it, she would talk to him.

When Donna talked to Uncle Rhett, he did not receive it well. He felt she was blaming him of something sinister and was completely offended. She enquired why he did not interact with the girls rather than just watch them and disappear into his room. Furious, he declared he did not know it was a crime to be proud of his niece and watch them. He stomped back to his room and slammed the door.

Robert had left on his vacation with Rain. He tried to remember the last time he and Donna had a great vacation together with unmerited fun. Probably before Chastain was born or perhaps longer. It did not matter. Donna did not have the love of life, unabashed fun and ability to live life to the fullest like Rain did. Rain was such a free spirit. Sometimes a bit too spirited but it was refreshing nonetheless. On the trip, Rain became upset. Robert wanted to kick back and relax a bit and she wanted to go shopping with him. As they fussed, she

PART II - Chastain

declared he probably should have stayed with Donna if he was going to live like a stick in the mud. He finally acquiesced and went with her. It was not a great day. She wanted many, many things and when he was not in agreement she would become argumentative and question his love for her. He spent considerable more money than he felt he should have but was glad the arguing stopped.

He had never noticed Rain being so flirtatious with so many men. Of course, most of their time before had been spent alone. She dressed in a provocative manner but that was what had first caught his attention. He felt he may be overreacting and paranoid. He wanted her all to himself. He did not want other men taking such notice of her. Why he not noticed such things before? And where did this sense of entitlement attitude come from? Had he just not noticed it before? Again, it was because the time they spent together sneaking around had been much different than now, living this flagrant life out loud.

At the next cheerleading practice Uncle Rhett brought a lawn chair and came out in the yard with the girls. He was great with instructions. He let them know if they were not lifting their legs high enough and even stood at the bottom of the pyramid giving instructions to each girl and making sure our top cheerleader had solid enough footing. When back in his chair with a cold drink, he did not say much but kept repositioning himself in his chair. The girls giggled and asked if he had ants in his pants or what. He didn't find their comments funny. It was not too long after that he picked up some pom poms telling the girls they did not need them right now so he would take them inside. He stacked them like a totem pole up his body. It was so funny looking. Later as the girls were getting ready to stop for the day, Chastain noticed her Uncle Rhett at the window again. What was the deal? As the girls came in the house, Chastain went to Rhett's bedroom door and told him that he could come have some refreshments with them. He thanked her for her offer but said he was busy at the moment. Maybe next time.

PART II - CHASTAIN

PART III
BIANCA

PART III - BIANCA

Now that they were living with Milo, they had to change schools again. Bianca dreaded it but hoped it would be better than the last experience. She now lived next a trailer park that seemed to have its very own distinct smell. It didn't smell like sewer or something rotten…she couldn't put her finger on what the odor was. There was a tall fence between their house and the trailer park. Trash lined the fence as far back as she could see.

As summer arrived Bianca noticed the fence line at the trailer park needed mowed and a weed-eater used on it. Milo's yard had sparse grass and a big tree in the middle with no grass around it. It was better than the last yard they had. Bianca thought of how much prettier the yard would be if they planted flowers around that big tree, maybe with a little fence around the flowers would make it perfect. She decided to ask her mom if that would be ok. It would be fun to go shop for some flowers.

That evening as Bianca was setting the table for supper, she brought it up. She explained to her mom how pretty she thought it would be and pleaded to get to flowers. Her mother had told her they would talk to Milo about it at dinner time. Milo was not as keen on the idea. He felt the flowers may not grow because they wouldn't get enough sun or that the neighborhood dogs would dig them up. After much talk about it, Annette reminded him that now he lived with three ladies and they would want to add a woman's touch to things. Milo leaned back in his chair stating he could not argue with that one bit and that it would be fine to plant the flowers as long as they could afford them. He had lost his job again and was currently looking for something else. It seemed to Bianca he had lost a few jobs since her family had met him. She decided she could be wrong, it could just seem that way because she may have been looking for fault in Milo because she wanted her mom and dad back together. Milo startled Bianca out of her reverie when he had reached over and placed his hand on her thigh. He was saying something about being more accommodating with Bianca becoming a woman and needing to spread her wings a bit and learn more about what they actually meant.

Waiting for the weekend, to go buy the flowers seemed like an eternity to Bianca. She had drawn pictures of what she wanted it to look like so she could choose the plan that would look the best. Finally, Saturday arrived and they

PART III - Bianca

loaded up in the car to see what they could find. Bianca picked out some Impatiens and Begonias. They were not supposed to require a lot of light so she thought they would be perfect! She could not wait to get home. She had decided a small fence would hide the beauty of her flowers so she decided against that. As she walked toward the register with her mother, Milo again noticed Bianca's sashay in her walk. It really was just like her mothers.

When they arrived back home, her mother instructed her to go put on some play clothes that would be okay to get dirty while she planted. As Bianca was dressing, she realized many of her clothes were too tight for her now. She picked out a mint green tank top that was rather fitted to her middle but a little looser at the chest and straps. Her shorts would no longer fit. She called for her mom to come help her. Annette decided they could cut off a pair of her jeans that still fit and make them shorts. Bianca was thankful for the resolution but wanted to get started on her plants right now. She overheard her mom telling Milo what the problem was. He kind of laughed and said Bianca was turning into a woman and going to have some hips men would love someday. Bianca did not find that statement funny. Why would men love her hips? She thought that was absurd. Her mother soon returned with the cut-off shorts. Bianca quickly changed and headed for the yard.

Planting the flowers in the hard ground was more of a process than Bianca thought it would be. She had to go and ask for help. Milo came out to help her dig up the places for her plants to go. He would dig it up and have her put the flowers in and cover them with dirt. At one point, as they were both squatted down, Milo said it was amazing how much she had grown in the time he had known her. She asked what he meant. He pointed to her top. She did not realize it was gaping open and was embarrassed as she pulled it to her chest. He told her not to worry about it, he had simply noticed they may need to get her some bigger bras. Bianca flushed beet red at the comment. She pulled her shirt down more in the back so it wouldn't fall open so far. She was very conscientious and kept tugging at her shirt as they finished up planting. The flowers looked beautiful and she was very proud.

Before Bianca knew it, they were getting ready to go back to school. Her dad got Aunt Demi to take the girls shopping for school clothes and necessities. Bianca had heard her

PART III - Bianca

mom on the phone saying she did not have the money to do it all and her dad said he would just take care of all of it. Aunt Demi made the shopping trip so much fun. They shopped most of the morning but did not have everything they needed so Aunt Demi took them to a nice restaurant for lunch. Bianca realized this was not something they ever did with their mom anymore. It was such a treat! After lunch, the shopping continued. Aunt Demi made the whole thing seem like a fashion show. Once they had finally finished up, the girls were still giggling and this time they went for ice cream to celebrate all the wonderful finds of the day. On the way home, Dana fell asleep almost as soon as the car started moving. Bianca asked her Aunt why she thought her mom never seemed to have any money and never took them out to eat anymore. Her Aunt politely shared she would need to ask her mom those questions because she did not have the answers. Bianca asked if Demi thought Milo was lazy or just always down on his luck. She felt it was a family problem as to why they rarely got to go do things. Again, as politely as she could, Demi refrained from speaking her true thoughts and simply said she had no idea because she did not actually know

Milo. At this point Aunt Demi was trying to think of anything/everything else to talk about. She asked Bianca if she had made new friends and about the new school she would be going to. How she felt about moving up to Jr. High next year? Demi was elated the conversation took a different turn. She could never tell her nieces how she really felt about their mother now much less that low down nasty Milo.

The fashion show resumed after dinner. The girls put on every outfit for their dad to see. He would laugh as they would dance around the living room or pirouette back down the hall. He thanked Demi profusely for being such a wonderful sister and aunt. He knew the girls adored her. Many times when he had picked the girls up their clothes didn't look very clean and they just did not appear happy the way he remembered them being when they were all still together. His thoughts wandered down that very narrow path that was filled with contempt for Annette and Milo. He had not cared for Milo when he first met him. He should have seen the signs of what was unfolding but obviously he had not recognized them. How he wished he had at times. Other times, he felt it was good riddance of Annette if that's the type of man

PART III - BIANCA

she really wanted. But then there were the kids. What kind of example were those two setting for his girls? He wanted to be sure he taught them how a man should treat them. He was certain that was not what they were currently seeing. Demi interrupted his thoughts by asking if he was okay. He told her yes, just some unpleasant thoughts had entered his mind. He told her that he greatly appreciated the interruption. He expressed there was just something about Milo he didn't trust and no reason to respect him. Demi agreed and told him they could have that conversation after the girls returned home. Those words pierced Damien like a hot knife. Home. This was their home.

When he returned the girls to their mother, he just could not help himself. He had to leave quickly due to the tears forming at his eyes due to the heartbreak he had given attention to last night after everyone had gone to bed. He still loved Annette but knew he needed to move on and give up the ghost of them being a happy family again. There was such a burning at the thought it really never was going to happen.

The girls were reinvigorated by the thought of another fashion show for their mom and Milo! They gave their dad a kiss with a rushed I love you as they got out of the car. They ran to the front door with their sacks of goodies.

Their mom told them she would love to see their fashion show! Milo grabbed a beer and plopped down in his chair. As the girls showed off their beautiful outfits, they came to a place of showing off their new dresses. Milo took a long slug off of his beer and told them to get back in there. He told them to face the tv and bend over. He explained he was making sure the dresses were not too short, especially for Bianca. Annette thought he was so wonderful to have thought of that. While the girls were changing, yet again, she told Milo she bet Damien had not had enough sense to check that. When they re-entered the room, Milo had them bend over yet again. Bianca was very uncomfortable and there were just times something about Milo felt very eerie. This was definitely one of those times. Then he actually asked her if she got new bras and panties! She turned beat red from the neck up, answered yes and ran back to her room totally embarrassed.

One morning mid summer Bianca noticed blood on her underwear. She did not know what was wrong. She went to her bedroom saying she just did not feel well and wanted to lay down.

PART III - Bianca

Her mom was not home and that was who she needed. She was not comfortable telling Milo something was wrong and what was going on. The truth was she did not feel comfortable telling anyone but knew she had to because something was definitely wrong with her. Once her mother came home Bianca called her to the bedroom. Through tears she told her mom what was going on. Her mother giggled. Bianca couldn't believe it. She could be dying and her mom giggled. Her mother explained to her about the menstruation cycle and that this would happen every month. She went and got some cramping reliever and a hot pad to put on her abdomen. Bianca was beside herself. She was going to do this every month from now on. Her mother said it was part of becoming a woman. Bianca did not like it but apparently couldn't change it either.either.

PART III
SYBIL

PART III - Sybil

Later, James woke up and stumbled into Sybil's room. He just stood there looking at her at first. She was sleeping. He went over to her bed and woke her, telling her to be very quiet so she would not wake her mom and brother. He laid beside her on the bed, touching her. This time he kept touching her between her thighs. He told her it was time to start learning lessons at home so she did not get knocked up and have to get married when she was older. He started rubbing himself against her leg and would brush his hand across her chest occasionally. He made some weird kind of noises and showed himself to her, saying first of all she needed to know what boys looked like because they were much different than girls. Sybil was scared and wanted him to stop. He rubbed against her some more, telling her there was so much more to learn. Finally he stopped and stumbled out of her room. She didn't want to learn about boys if that was how different they were. Plus, she could still smell the beer from his breath and it stunk.

    The day finally came that Gail was born. William and Gayla were over the moon in love with her. Sybil went to the hospital with her mom to see them. She was amazed at how little

Gail was. She was smaller than some of her own baby dolls! She had big eyes and some dark hair. She was currently sporting a big pink bow. Upon returning home, Athena told James about Gail. He did not pay very much attention. Then he asked if Sybil went to. Sybil was scared she was in trouble. Athena told him, Sybil had gone and got to hold the baby as well. James laughed, turning to Sybil then asked if they had told her where that baby came from. Sybil said no sir, a little frightened. He said that place between your legs you thought was a bad place, well it's a bad place when you're pushing a baby out of it. Think about that. That's why you have to learn so it does not happen to you. He grabbed a beer and went into the living room. Sybil was looking at her mother wide-eyed and asked if that was really where Gail had come from. Athena was furious with James for saying that! Now it was left to her to try to explain a bit about having a baby. This was not a conversation she had planned to have for a couple more years. When Sybil went to bed, she laid there thinking about what she had learned today. It was really gross to her. And she definitely didn't want that to happen to her, no matter how much her mom said the body would change to make it

PART III - Sybil

possible. Yuck!

The following week, her mom was gone to a meeting and she was home with her dad. He had her go into her room where he did the same thing he had done before. Sybil didn't like it but didn't want a baby coming out either!

Mason pretty much did his own thing. He was not home very often. He had a job after school and a girlfriend. Her dad complained about the girlfriend but her mom would remind him that Mason had grown up quite a bit and she was sure he would make good decisions when it came to her. She explained that his job kept him very busy as well. She felt sure he had learned lessons from William's experience.

Once in a while, James would ask how Gail was doing. He never went to see her or anything, but would ask. Athena hoped that was a good step to eventually mending his relationship with William.

William enlisted and was leaving for basic training soon. Athena wanted to be able to help Gayla with Gail but was not sure how possible that would be.

One day Athena came home crying. It was about their grandparents in Georgia. Grandpa was sick and not doing well. Grandma wasn't sure she could take care of him the way she needed to and was contemplating the need to place him in a nursing home. Athena was taking vacation time to go see about them and what needed to be done. She was a tad surprised James did not argue with her. She packed that night and left the next morning. Sybil gave her mom one of her homemade flowers to give to Grandma and kissed her mom goodbye. From the first night her mom was gone, Sybil's life was changed. Her dad had other things for them to do during her mom's absence. None of it was fun. She learned more about womanhood and what a man's body does than she wanted to know. She would cry and cry afterwards. It was horrible and made her feel dirty. She always had to go wash off afterwards.

At school, Sybil made a new friend that lived a couple miles from her home. She wanted to stay at her house the next Friday night. Her father told her if she was a very good girl, he would let her go. No tears, no fighting him, and no throwing up. Sybil was not sure she could be that good but she would try. She really wanted to stay at her friends house all night.

On Friday night, Sybil's dad took her over to Samantha's house. The girls had a great time.

PART III - Sybil

When they went to bed Samantha asked Sybil if she had ever touched anyone else without their clothes on. Sybil answered no. At first she was afraid somehow Samantha knew what she was already learning. She knew that could not be though, because no-one knew. Sybil felt safe doing this with a girl. She wasn't capable of doing the gross things a boy could. The girls stayed at each others house as often as they could and would engage in this activity. For the life of them, they couldn't figure out why boys liked it so much. One night Sybil taught Samantha about not doing things with boys before she got married because they would make her push a baby out of her privates. Samantha was shocked by this new information. She was unaware that's how you got a baby!

Athena was dismayed at how bad her father really was doing. She discussed home health care with the Dr. and they both ended up agreeing that it would not be enough care for his needs. Her mother's health was failing. She was having great difficulty getting around with a walker and had become very absent minded. Forgetting she had put the tea kettle on the stove, not locking the doors at night, and various other things. Athena talked to her about both of them going into a home so they would both receive the care they needed. She tried to be upbeat about it and make it sound great by telling her mom she could go to Bingo, get her nails/hair done, play cards and make some great new friends. Although all those things were truth, it broke Athena's heart. Athena went and checked out a few nursing homes and assisted care facilities. Her dad was too ill for assisted living. She did find a very beautiful place for them. She spoke with the Activities Director about keeping her mom busy and types of activities they did. She set up an appointment to come back the next day with her mother. Although Athena knew it was for the best, it hurt.

She called Logan, Sebastian and Davina to discuss it with them. They were unable to get there at the time, for various reasons. They talked at length about what would be prime for their parents. There were tears with each call. It was the worst with Davina. She cried over her mom and dad. She cried because she was not there to help. She cried because Athena was doing this all alone. Athena assured her, she had shed many tears as well. The kids were all in agreement about what to do.

Her mother really liked the nursing home.

PART III - Sybil

She especially liked the activities director and all the things she told about that there was to do. She did giggle and say it would kind of be nice not to do her own cooking and cleaning. They got Dr's orders and made arrangements to move them in the following week. Athena was feeling overwhelmed just thinking about what to do with all their stuff. She would have to go through everything to ensure they had what they needed. She was going to need a storage shed for now until they could have an estate sale, then sell the house. They would have to get together and paint and do what work was needed to spruce up the house or hire someone to do it. She would discuss all of that with her brothers and sister later.

 Back at home Sybil was loving her newfound friendship. Being good with her father was becoming easier. At least she no longer threw up anymore. Samantha was staying at Sybil's house the next weekend. They now told people they were sisters.

 When the weekend arrived the girls were ecstatic! They couldn't wait to get to Sybil's. Her father had even taken her shopping for her weekend with Samantha! It has cost her an extra session of being good but Samantha was worth it. The girls played barbies most of the evening. Mason came through on his dinner break and stepped in and said hello. They wanted to share snacks with him, so he sat down at their little table and had snacks along with soda. They were too cute together. Mason ruffled Sybil's hair as he got up to leave. Sybil knew he was making plans to move out but she tried not to think about it.

    Late the first night, Samantha told Sybil she had started a new thing! When she would get hurt in the private place, afterward she would take the eraser on a pencil and grind it into her leg until the pain made her not think about it anymore. She showed Sybil how she did it. Sybil was confused but did not ask why the private place would hurt. She did not want Samantha to think she was stupid.

    Sybil had found a Ouija board in Williams closet and the girls got it out. They would ask if a certain boy liked them, if winter would be cold, were they considered young ladies yet, etc. They both swore the other one was pushing the heart shaped piece of wood around the board. They laughed and had a pillow fight before getting ready for bed. They had demonstrated to each other what they wanted to do under the covers

PART III - SYBIL

that night with the barbie dolls. Sybil was afraid her dad would catch them. Samantha assured her they would be very quiet so he would not have a reason to check on them. The next night was more of the same.

PART III
Chastain

PART III - CHASTAIN

Day, weeks, then months rolled by and Donna was still a mess. She was still in awe that her husband left her for a younger woman. After all these years, how dare he? She was quite certain Rain was in it for the money, but, Robert was too wrapped up in it to see it. She was not nice to Chastain. Not that she was outright mean to her. Chastain had come home from her dad's more than once upset that Rain refers to her as 'her' or 'the girl'. It was noticeable she did not want her around. Why couldn't Robert see it? For that matter, why couldn't Robert see anything immediately around him other than Rain? Just the thought of it made her furious all over again.

Uncle Rhett was becoming more friendly with Chastain. He would express concern and tell her, she could always talk to him. Chastain began to feel all alone with her dad gone and her mom not accepting it well at all. She felt she had no-one. Sure, she had friends but they were to the point of just telling her to suck it up and move on. It was very hurtful.

Once a month or so, Grandpa would come over and play chess with her. She loved the game. She had dreams of being a champion, among the elite chess players. Sometimes she felt she lived for the challenges of the game. Her friends were not into chess and thought it was boring. They did not understand the strategy you had to use. Strange how a board and its pieces could captivate you.

Donna did not feel comfortable at the Country Club. She always felt like the women were whispering about her and what happened to her marriage. She did not want their pity. She wanted them to be the same friends to her they had been before all of this happened. She knew some of the ladies and their husbands had been to the new condo for the lavish parties Rain threw. It always made her want to cry every single time. A few of the ladies were still her good friends and they took her side in what they referred to as an awful mess. They also felt Robert was throwing his life away. Maybe that was what it was. She needed people in her boat that felt the same way about all of this that she did.

Chastain had entered Junior High. Sometimes Donna would sit and go through pictures as she wondered how the time had gone by so fast. Chastain had begun to open up to her Uncle Rhett, sometimes even spending time in his room with him. Donna knew there

PART III - CHASTAIN

were times Chastain felt unloved and tossed aside. Yet another reason, all of this got to Donna so much. Donna wanted to be there for her but would find herself only wanting to spew harsh comments about her father. Therefore, Donna tried to avoid the conversations. Donna had been placed on antidepressants and anti-anxiety meds. She hated that she needed to take them. Most of the time she did not feel they were working. She spent a lot of time in her room crying or sleeping. Should this be lasting this long? Shouldn't the medication have made her go back to her normal self? Everything felt like a major feat to accomplish.

Robert and Rain were having some difficult times. Rain's entitlement was getting out of hand. Most of the time they would argue, Rain would leave, go party with friends, then return and apologize. For a time, all would go well, then the cycle would repeat itself. To the public, they always put on a great show and you would never know they had issues. Many of Robert's friends would tell him how jealous they were and wished they could find someone like Rain to fall for them. Sometimes, Robert would smile but it was because on the inside he was thinking that it wasn't all it was cracked up to be a lot of the time.

Robert noticed Chastain was looking like she had lost weight since her clothes seemed to be rather baggy on her. Oversized shirts, loose pants and her face looked thin. He asked her about it and she acted like she did not know what he was talking about. The truth was she was not eating much anymore and would throw up many times when she did. There were things going on in her life no-one would understand or care about. She tried not to, but whether or not she ate, how much she allowed herself to eat were all things she had control over. She felt everything else was out of control and she would go crazy. This made her feel better about herself. She was hiding things out of shame. How could she ever explain any of it to her dad? He made the choice to leave her so it was not like he would really care.

Chastian's mother finally noticed her weight loss as well and began to cook and bake more often. Donna blamed it all on Robert. Truth be told, there was not much she didn't blame Robert for. He caused this whole mess. She was surprised at herself for not noticing Chastain's weight loss. When Donna cooked, Chaistain always ate so she didn't understand.

PART III - Chastain

And why hadn't Chastain said anything?

Uncle Rhett was very pleased with the progress he had made with Chastain. With the vulnerable state she was in, it really wasn't all that difficult to chastise her into doing what he wanted. She needed to feel loved. She wasn't always agreeable and it was gut wrenching when she would cry. He knew when she was younger he would have her one day. It had happened sooner than he had thought. He knew it wasn't right but he didn't care, he simply wanted her. Someday he would have her completely. Maybe she would see she needed him and would understand she was always meant for him. He would own her one day. He had told her that. He sure hoped she understood he would never stop coming after her. What they were doing was nothing compared to what he wanted to do. He had girlfriends from time to time but it never lasted. They were always on him about his need to pay once in a while. He just could not seem to understand he needed a job to pay for dates and those were hard to come by. He resented his brother for not giving him a job. Sure he always gave him a place to stay, with food and time around Chastain but a job would have been good too. They had argued more than once about it. Robert did not believe he could become an agent and handle the job. He would show him! Once Robert made the decision to leave, it left the door wide open for Rhett to get to Chastain. Once she had started all that cheerleading did him in. He knew he had to have her in one fashion or another. Robert just made it easier in every way.

Chastain was becoming less involved in things at school. She had this hate inside of her that she was not sure where it was coming from. Originally, she knew it was at her father. Then it was at her uncle. Maybe it was becoming more daunting because it was a hate for both of them. Rain had ruined their entire lives. Uncle Rhett would not have ever started doing the things he was doing to her. She felt like scum but did not know what to do. How do you tell someone that your uncle is molesting you? It all started with him acting like he truly cared about her and what she was going through with her parents. Her dad was too wrapped up in Rain to care. Her mom always seemed on the verge of a breakdown due to the whole situation. Chastain could not help being mad at her mom as well. She needed her mom and dad and had neither. She was amazed at how easy it was to

PART III - CHASTAIN

just push the food on her plate around a little bit and it looked like she had eaten. She always told her mom how delicious it was but that she just could not eat it all and would whisk the plate away and dump it in the trash. She would be starting in the Chess Club but it was not soon enough. She had been studying about the game and strategies.

Donna's women's group was going to start getting together another night of the week for a bible study. It did not particularly sound like anything she would be interested in. She was so mad at God for letting her husband leave her! The ladies passed out little flyers with all the information for those who wanted to attend. One of them asked Donna if she was going to come. She told her not this time, she just had so much on her plate she just could not fit it in. Why did people having a bible study group offend her so much? She was acting ridiculous.

In reality, Donna was doing much better but there were just times she wanted her husband home. She would make herself crazy thinking of all the things he was doing with Rain. It was like a fresh, new wound every time she put herself through that and yet she could not seem to stop. She could not stop questioning herself about what she had done wrong either. Sometimes she would sit and think of how she would do things different if she had Robert back. Donna sensed Chastain drawing further and further away and didn't have a clue how to change it. She knew she was at fault in the way she handled, or didn't handle was more like it, Robert leaving. She was going to make a point to do some things with her like they used to.

Unfortunately for Chastain and Donna, Rhett was just feeling right at home. It was obvious he did not plan to go away anytime soon. He did spend a lot of time in the guest room, but Donna just dreaded when he would be with her and Chastain. The only good that had come out of it was his relationship with his niece. Donna knew Chastain had turned to him out of desperation. One parent gone, the other basically gone for much longer than she should have been. She had been in such pain. She did not realize how much she loved Robert and the hole in her heart was still quite large. She did not understand why he had not filed for divorce yet. What was he waiting for?

Later that week, Donna made plans to take Chastain to the Country Club and an afternoon at the spa. That should make them both feel

PART III - Chastain

better for a while. When they went to lunch, there was a delicious salad on the menu and she kept urging Chastain to order it but she was not having it at all. Donna was getting very concerned with Chastain's weight loss. She let her order whatever she wanted. Chastain cut her chicken into tiny little pieces so she wouldn't have to eat so much but it would look like she was. She just felt huge when she ate and she despised that feeling. If she could just drop about 10 more pounds, she would be happy. She ate more than she had planned. She was mortified with herself and the thought she was going to look fat at the spa. She excused herself, went to one of the restrooms and made herself throw up. When she looked at herself in the mirror, she felt accomplished because that food was not going to put more weight on her. Of course, Donna was oblivious to what she had just done.

Chastain passed on desert, saying she was too full for one more bite of anything. When her mother finished, they headed for the spa. Chastain was looking forward to it. Maybe she could feel like herself instead of feeling Uncle Rhett against her. No matter how hard she scrubbed when she showered, she still felt dirty. The afternoon was wonderful for both of them. Being pampered and relaxed suited both of them just fine. They both hated the fact it was time to go. They both had to admit, it was a great day overall.

    Robert called that evening and wanted to pick Chastain up for the weekend. She did not see near as much of her dad as she had thought she would. She jumped at the chance even though she knew it would make her mom sad and Rain would probably be rude. She wished she could just have a daddy-daughter day. As it turned out, Saturday kind of was a daddy - daughter day. They played chess and Chastain could not hide her enthusiasm. Rain left to go get a manicure and pedicure so it was even better since it was jus the two of them. This was the first time they had played Chess since he had left. He had to admit, Chastain was quite the little opponent. She gave him a good run. They were in their second game when Rain returned. She wanted to know how much longer they were going to just sit there and stare at that stupid board. Chastain couldn't help herself and rolled her eyes. She was very certain Rain was not capable of such an intelligent game. Rain had not noticed the roll of the eyes and Chastain

PART III - Chastain

was glad. It would have got something started and they would not have been able to finish this game. Rain came back through later demanding Robert get up from that stupid board. She wanted to go do something, anything, just not this. She thought they should take Chastain shopping for new clothes. Chastain didn't want to go anywhere else, she loved the moment she was in. Rain became very upset when Robert dismissed her and told her to go to the Country Club or lay out by the pool. This started an argument. She wanted his undivided attention and was actually throwing a fit about it. She had raised her voice and used some obscenities before Robert jumped up. grabbed her by the arm. and escorted her into another room. Chastain did not know what went on there but when they came out, Rain was fuming. She glared at Chastain and told her she hoped she was happy, coming over and ruining her whole life. Robert interrupted and told her that was enough and to go on about her day. When Rain left, Robert apologized to Chastain. That was the first time that had happened since he moved out. They finished their second game and were mentally exhausted. They changed clothes and headed for the pool.

The next day was good other than putting up with Rain's pouting. She was not allowed to have a party this weekend due to Chastain being there. As she put it, she just felt completely out of sorts without their friends around. Robert pointed out the obvious: they did not need people over every single weekend. Rain actually began to cry. Chastain had never seen anyone act like such a big baby all the time. Later, Robert took Chastain home. On the way, he asked her how she was doing. He was very worried about her physical appearance of obvious too much weight loss. She simply dismissed it and told him a few less pounds had never hurt anyone. Then she jokingly told him, he might want to try it. They arrived laughing. Donna happened to be outside. He thought it peculiar that he would notice how beautiful she was. Chastain hopped out of the car. Robert found himself wishing Donna would come over and say hello. He felt like it would be offbeat for him to get out of the car and go chat. Why would she want to after all he had put her through. He simply waved and backed out of the drive.

PART III - CHASTAIN

PART IV
BIANCA

PART IV - Bianca

The next evening at dinner, Milo asked her how she was doing with becoming a woman. Bianca was mortified. Her mom had told him what was happening? Why would she do that? Didn't she think it was embarrassing enough? Bianca barely ate and went immediately to her room and cried. She wished she had told Aunt Demi instead. At least she wouldn't have told the whole world about her business.

Annette's idea had been to quit her job and devote all of her attention to Milo once they got moved in and settled. She had put in her notice and left her job. At that time, Milo was working catered events. That only lasted a short time. Then, neither of them had a job, and they began the process of getting assistance. Milo still had not found a job, and Annette knew they needed to do something, so she took a job as a waitress. She had liked her career as a secretary better, but the tips were good. She would do whatever it took for her and Milo to be happy. She felt terrible that he had not been able to find a good job. She had hoped the city would hire him to work in the sanitation department but two weeks had passed with no word.

Milo and one of his friends, Leonard, decided to start a mowing company and take care of yards for money. Leonard was so much like him they could have been related. He also liked to sit around, drink beer, and watch tv. Every now and then, he and Milo would go down to the basement and Bianca would take care of Dana. Those nights seemed more relaxed. She could play a game, have a tea party, or play dolls with Dana before helping her get ready for bed. She wished there were more nights like this.

Being left at home with Milo just seemed weird to Bianca. Dana was happy to get to play a game with him, but most of the time he only drank beer and watched tv. A couple times now he had walked into the bathroom while Bianca was in the bath. She couldn't cover herself enough when this happened, and she was very uneasy, so she spoke to her mom. Annette was outraged that Bianca whined about every little thing when it came to Milo. Annette told her if she thought causing all these problems were going to land her back at her dad's, she was wrong. They needed her there for the assistance they were receiving, and that would not change. She told Bianca to get over it and quit being a baby. It broke Bianca's heart, and she wondered if she was really being a baby.

PART IV - Bianca

School began, and Bianca felt odd knowing she was going to school as a woman. She was not sure that actually made a difference, but she was not going to tell anyone about it. She met some kids that had older siblings in school. They would invite her over or to go places with them but usually, she could not. She had to walk over and get Dana at school and walk home with her. In one way she kind of resented it because her mother was home in the afternoon and Bianca wanted to go do things with the other kids her age. She wondered if Dana had adjusted so well because she was so young. Her father was busy working most of the time so they did not get to see him near as much as Bianca would have liked for them too.

Finally, Bianca was going to get to go to a movie with her friends! She was beside herself with joy. Her friend, Natalee, had an older brother and he was going to take them and bring them home. When they left, Natalee's brother told them he needed to pick up a friend real quick. Once they had picked him up, he lit a cigarette. It did not bother Bianca because Milo smoked all the time. But it didn't smell right. Then he gave it to Natalee's brother. They were both smoking the same cigarette. She asked Natalee why. Natalee giggled and told her the boys were smoking pot. Bianca had heard of marijuana but had never been around it before. When they arrived at the movie, Bianca was surprised the boys were going to leave to pick up some girls. She thought they were all going to stay together until she was taken back home.

The boys showed up late. The movie had been over for 20 minutes, leaving Natalee and Bianca just standing outside until they showed up. Bianca did not want to get into trouble the first time she got to go out. Unanticipated, Milo was much more upset than her mom was. Her mom sent her to get ready for bed. Afterward, they talked about the movie then hung out in the living room and watched tv. Milo was still very unhappy. Her mom told her not to be concerned, he had probably just had one too many beers.

The following week, while Annette was at work, things took a very odd turn at home. Dana was asleep, she had an earlier bedtime than Bianca. After Bianca had gone to her room and climbed into bed, her door slowly opened, and she could see the faint glow of the tv. It was Milo. He sat on the bed and asked if she had sex with her friend's brother. She explained she

PART IV - Bianca

only went to the movie and home. Milo told her, she needed to learn about sex before having it, and as the man of the house, it was his job to help her mom out with that. He pushed her onto her stomach and laid on her. Not wholly, one arm was holding up his upper body. Bianca wasn't sure what was going on, she didn't like it and asked him to stop. After a couple of grunts, he stopped and went back into the living room. This became the 'normal' for several weeks.

One day while her mom was home, Milo clarified that it was their job as parents to teach Bianca about sex. Her mother ultimately agreed and told Bianca this was something that needed to be learned at home, so she knew facts and not what kids were guessing that it was. This weighed on Bianca. She was not sure she even wanted to know about sex and hoped it did not have anything to do with what Milo got on her leg the other night. However, they are the adults that make the rules. Who was Bianca to argue? She knew it would not get her anywhere and would probably just get her grounded.

Then it happened. One night Milo came to her room and told her to come down to the basement with him. She inquired as to why they were going down there. She and Dana had not been allowed down there. He informed her that Dana had nothing to do with it. This was about her learning about sex. Upon entering the basement, the tv had something terrible on it that Bianca had never seen. Why were they watching this? She turned her back to it. Milo looked her over and told her to get undressed. When she asked why he replied to her that he had talked to her mom about both of them teaching her about sex, and this is where they would start. Bianca could hear the strange sounds coming from the tv. She was very disturbed by the show and wanted Milo to turn it off. He refused saying it would help the process and was also a teaching tool. He gruffly demanded she get undressed. She was very embarrassed when she was removing her nightgown. He showed her what he had been doing on the nights he had come to her room. She was even more embarrassed that he was undressed. He touched her in ways she didn't like, but her mom had already told her it was ok and indeed she had said they would both teach her about proper sex. She didn't know why he looked at her the way he did. Again, the noises the people on TV were making in the background! What he had gotten on her leg

PART IV - Bianca

previously definitely had to do with her training because it happened again. She thought it was so gross. He cleaned her up and sent her back to her room. He stopped her and reminded her that this was his area. She was only allowed to be down here for her lessons, and he would let her know when that was. Bianca practically ran up the stairs to her room. She didn't want to learn if this was what it consisted of. She tried to tell her mom, but she had already done that to no avail. She felt trapped. She cried until she fell asleep.

    She and her friend Natalee became best friends. When Bianca's mom was home, Natalee was allowed to come over. There were times she got to go to Natalee's as well. Natalee couldn't stay all night, and Bianca was not allowed to stay over with Natalee on nights Bianca's mom worked. Annette told her she was the woman of the house when her mama was gone, and she needed Bianca to take care of all the things she would normally do.

    Soon, the trips to the basement were every night Annette was not home. Things had moved forward in her lessons, and now Milo was going to teach her real sex. Bianca cried out loud at the pain, but it didn't phase Milo. He always had that tv playing with those shows on it. Everything seemed deafening between the pain and the sounds from the tv. Sometimes Milo reeked of alcohol and the smell made her stomach turn. The things that were going on in that basement were anything but fun.

Fall had ended, so Milo and Leonard had no work. For the most part, they just hung around the house or hung out in the basement. When he was working, they had continued to get assistance. He said most of his customers were cash customers anyway and that it would be easier than reapplying when the work dried up for the winter. Occasionally, when Annette was home, she would have Bianca watch Dana, and the three of them would go to the basement. Again, these times seemed peaceful.

Bianca and Dana had gone to see their dad a few times, but it definitely was not every other weekend. Her father had stocked needed items for menstruation in case she ever needed them when she was at his house. Bianca was mortified. Had her mother told everyone in the world? How embarrassing to know her dad knew as well.

On this particular visit, they were going out to dinner to meet a friend of their dad's. The

PART IV - BIANCA

friend was a she! Bianca didn't like it. Milo had taken her mom, was this woman going to take her dad? Dana was pleased as she interacted with Angi. Angi helped her color her picture on the back of the child's menu. She seemed very pleasant, but Bianca still felt threatened. After supper, they walked down the street to an ice cream shop for dessert. Angi seemed very interested in Bianca and her likes and dislikes. That was refreshing. Angi asked her about school, her classes, friends etc. Bianca was hoping she was not going to bring up her becoming a woman. Why in the world did any woman like what women did? She certainly was not going to ask, she was already very self-conscience about all the changes in her life since summer. As Bianca thought about it, this was a lovely evening, and Angi did seem exceptionally nice. According to the exchange taking place, Angi had known Damien since just before school started. Bianca began to quiz Angi about going on dates with her dad. Angi's eyes lit up as she talked of what a gentleman Damien was, and some places they had gone. It dawned on Bianca that she didn't remember seeing that spark in her mom's eye in a while. Or was it there and she had not noticed as she had been so focused on becoming a woman and all that entailed?

After ice cream, they walked Angi back to her car. Bianca noticed that her dad had opened the door for her, made sure she was in and shut it for her. She found that very interesting. Overall, she had to admit Angi did seem really nice. Her dad was smiling ear to ear as he walked back to Bianca and Dana asking what they thought of Angi. They chatted about her on the way home. He tried to express how important it was to him that they like anyone who was in his life and that person, referring to Angi, could not take their place. He explained the girls were his baby girls and always would be and no-one could change that.

PART IV - Bianca

PART IV
SYBIL

PART IV - Sybil

Athena had to ask for a couple extra days off work to get everything settled with her parents. Her boss graciously agreed. This had all taken quite the toll emotionally on her. Once everything was taken care of, and she had been able to go visit her parents each day, she was feeling better. One afternoon, her mom told her it was great to see her, but it was time for aerobics, and she could not miss that. Athena was thrilled her mom was enjoying her new home. Her father was doing better now that he was getting better care and medications when he needed them.

Athena made the drive back home with a much lighter heart than what it had been. She was positive her brothers and sister would approve of the home their parents were in and the arrangements she made for some yard/pest control that was much needed. She was excited to get home to her husband and children. She hoped they had missed her as much as she did them.

The night before Athena came home, James made two trips to Sybil's room. He told her lessons would not be as much now because she had done so well. Sybil was so glad to hear this. She still felt sick to her stomach even though she was no longer throwing up.

Her mom arrived home, and Sybil ran to the car to meet her! She helped carry her mom's bags in talking a mile a minute about her newfound friend Samantha. After getting in the house, Sybil apologized as she realized she did not ask about her grandparents first. Athena shared with James and Sybil what had taken place and what will still need to be done. She was happy to share how well both of her parents were doing in their new home.

As time passed, Sybil's friendship with Samantha grew as did their exploits. One Sunday evening after returning from Samantha's, Sybil arrived home, and her mom was out. Her dad said she probably went to visit Gayla and Gail. He was on the couch, watching tv, drinking beer. Mason came through and headed right back out to go see his girlfriend. Sybil went back to her room to put up her belongings after her weekend stay. Shortly, her dad appeared in the doorway, leaning against it. He told her how she sure was growing up, and he swaggered into the room. He started in, saying they would just have a little wrestling fun. The same old stuff started in. Athena arrived back home, but James did not hear her. She entered the living room, not seeing

PART IV - Sybil

anyone there she immediately headed for Sybil's room. The door was half closed so she pushed it open and she could not believe what she was seeing. Her head began to spin as she asked James just what in the world he was doing! He immediately got up from Sybil who had started to cry. James grabbed Athena by the arm to pull her into another room, and Sybil cried out for her mother. Athena stopped and simply asked Sybil what she had done and to just stay in her room for the rest of the evening.

James tried to explain it must have been the beer, and he had not realized what he had done until Athena walked in. Athena demanded to know how long this had been going on. James told her that it wasn't a 'thing' much less a regular one. He blamed Sybil for looking so grown up and so much like her mother. He uttered he must have mistaken her for Athena. She had to admit since Sybil had entered Jr. High, she had gone through many changes. Puberty had certainly made her look more grown up. But could James have really mistaken her for Athena? She did not know what to think or believe as she began to cry. Oddly enough, one part of her wanted to go and check on Sybil, and another part was mad at her. She was old enough to know better! Why would she have let this happen? Maybe...maybe what? She did not know what to think and had no clarity at the moment. James came over and wrapped his arms around her saying he knew he was not always the best husband, but he would not purposely try to end all their years together.

Sybil cried out for her mom. Athena went to the door and just stood there looking at her. She had to admit her baby was growing up. She could not stop being mad at her. When Sybil asked to please come out of her room, Athena told her no. She said she had done enough for one day and she would bring her something to eat in a bit.

Later, when Sybil peeked out the door, her mom and dad were on the couch playing grown-up games. She was glad to see it this time. That must have meant everything was ok. Her mom was even drinking beer with her dad, which was unusual. Customarily her mom drank wine. Things must be a lot better! She was so relieved. Her mom had always told her that her dad would never hurt her. Maybe she was just surprised to see what was going on.

Sybil and Samantha had turned more of their attention to boys. Samantha had started being quite promiscuous and made it sound so

PART IV - Sybil

great to Sybil. Sybil was not convinced it was all that great yet. Samantha had done some things that seemed rather gross to Sybil. Samantha tried to explain they needed to try things in order to become real women. Their relationship had changed a bit since they had both developed. Everything seemed more sensitive.

A new boy had started going to their school, and Sybil thought he was just dreamy handsome. When he would say hello she would look off and murmur hello back. One day he had caught her in the hall and asked if they could go to a movie or something sometime. She explained she was not allowed to date yet. He told her that would still be okay, they could just meet up somewhere. He looked and acted like he should have been in High School.

Sybil could not contain her enthusiasm as she told Samantha about it. Samantha told her they could go and meet the boys one night when she stayed over. When they were at Sybil's house, they would say they were going to the mall or something and go see them. Samantha's boyfriend was in the 10th grade and had a pickup. Sybil laughed at her own excitement. However, they worked it out, they just always needed to be home on time.

Mason moved out. He had stayed around much longer than anticipated but decided to save money so he could have nice things. Sybil missed him but could go and see him when her mom would take her to his house. It was intriguing as the house was large and had a beautiful yard. The back yard had a large tree with a swing attached to a limb. Mason told Sybil she would always be the baby of the family, so he was leaving it there for her. She laughed because it was big enough to seat both of them and she said so. Out the door they ran to get on the swing like a couple of little kids. Athena loved the way Mason and Sybil had always been so close, and this made her heart fill with joy.

William and Gayla had moved. They lived a life of travel and new destinations every so often with William in the Service. Gail had gotten so big. Athena missed them terribly, but he was a grown man with a family doing what he loved, and the thought of that made her fulfilled. Athena did not have babies anymore, but all of her kids would always be her babies, no matter how old they got.

A few weeks later, Sybil and Samantha got the chance to meet up with the boys. They all went to a movie together. Samantha made Sybil

PART IV - Sybil

a little uncomfortable with all the kissing they were doing, but overall, it was a great evening. They made plans for later that night where the girls would climb out the bedroom window and meet back up with them in the backyard. That way, they could answer if Samantha's mom called out for them and would not think anything of them just being in the back yard.

James and Athena seemed to be getting along better than Sybil could ever recall. They actually went out on a few dates. Sybil did not recall that happening before, that she could remember. By now, Sybil knew what her dad was doing to her was wrong, but what could she do? Her mom knew and did nothing. Sybil thought about telling someone, but the things that happened were so embarrassing. It made her feel filthy and ashamed. She could not even tell Samantha. She was afraid it would ruin their friendship. She would not blame Samantha for thinking she was disgusting. She thought she was too. As much as she loved her parents, a small part of her hated them as well. Sybil had begun using the pencil eraser burn on her arms to kill the pain of the whole situation. She hated to admit she had thought of suicide. Wouldn't it be better than enduring this treatment at home?

A few times she had even begun writing a letter explaining why she had to leave and that the end of her life was the best thing for everyone. Each time, she would wind up shredding the letter because she could not act on it. The desire was there. The ability to do it was not. She had even gone to see if her dad's gun had bullets in it and if she could find some. She would hold the gun, even try putting it to her head but she just could not pull the trigger. One thing she promised herself was whenever she did have children, they would never get to wrestle. She hated the word itself…wrestle. It made her skin crawl. It is how all this got started. The only thing she really wanted was someone that would love, care, and protect her. Was that really too much to ask? Or was it not accessible to her for being so unworthy and dirty? Used…that's the word that kept coming to mind. Who would want her if they knew the truth? She would have to take this to the grave with her. Ultimately the burn of the pencil eraser wasn't enough, and she tried using a knife to cause the pain to go away. At first, it was just a prick, and that was enough pain to make her forget her problems. It worked for now at least.

PART IV - Sybil

PART IV
CHASTAIN

PART IV - Chastain

He was thinking about Donna on his way home. In reality, he realized he was comparing Donna and Rain. There simply was no comparison other than both women were stunning. He became lost in his thoughts as he drove. He found himself stopping at a pub he hadn't been to in years. He just needed to be alone with his thoughts before he returned home. He really didn't care that Rain would start blowing his phone up soon. He shut it off. When was the last time he just spent some alone time? He couldn't remember. Truth be told, he was kind of wishing he had never left to begin with. He did not know what he had been thinking. Obviously, he hadn't been. He candidly admitted to himself, he has just become enraptured with Rain. Looking back, he had everything a man could have wanted. Sure Donna was not as young as Rain, but she had a beautiful, natural sophistication about her. At dinner parties, Donna would never have gotten smashed out of her gourd and been a complete embarrassment. Donna would always whisper she was getting a bit heady when she had too much and would begin drinking water. There were so many thoughts swirling around in his head. Reasons to stay. Reasons to leave. Where was the happy medium? Or had he given it up for nothing? He had gotten so lost in thoughts, he didn't realize what time it was. He had been sitting in there for just over two hours. He flipped his phone back on. Several messages and missed calls from Rain. Great, this is precisely what he needed. Listening to her rant, call him inconsiderate, of cheating on her, etc. With the expenses of her, who could afford to have someone else. She could be downright ridiculous at times. And the bottom line was it was his own fault. He paid his tab and left.

Chastain went on and on about getting to play chess over the weekend. This was so effortful to have to listen to how good she thought he was. She was glad he had made the time though. Chastain needed it. Maybe she would start eating more. At this point, Donna had been thinking she might need to take Chastain to a therapist. Something was not right. She just could not figure out what it was. Rhett came through and gave Chastain a hug from the side. He was glad she was home. Her demeanor changed. She did not want him in there disrupting while she was retelling the wonderful time she had. Rhett asked her how Robert was doing these days. She only said the

PART IV - CHASTAIN

word, fine. Rhett wanted to know if he was still living like a kid or had he decided to be an adult yet. Chastain retorted, whatever, and took her things into her room. She waited until he left the kitchen before going back in to talk with her mom.

Rain was definitely not a picnic to handle when Robert got home. There was the obligatory yelling, some accusing and of course her concern of missing plans with friends that night. He did not want to go. When he told her, she was outraged at him. Telling him to go shower and get dressed right this minute. Her justification was the horrible weekend she had just endured, and he owed her. Something about that went all over him. He 'owed' her? For that, she was going alone. He'd had it with all these childish ways. She threatened him, letting him know she could not be held responsible for her actions if he refused to attend. He responded that he would take his chances. She stormed out the door, slamming it as hard as she could. Interesting that a picture of the two of them had fallen off the wall and broke. It summed up how he was feeling lately. This was a perfectly pictured painting of life.

Would Donna even consider letting him come home? He had made the worst of mistakes. His wife loved and adored him while he threw it all away. He had taken her for granted. The vacation…sure it would have been different but when was the last time he had made time for Donna, much less surprised her with a lavish vacation? Donna was purposeful in taking care of bills and expenses. She was not excessive. Then it hit him…he had gotten comfortable. He felt like such a loser. Why couldn't he see all of this before now? Maybe Donna did not have the perfect body , but she had also bored him their precious Chastain. Like time had not taken a toll on his physique as well. Donna did not care. She thought he was distinguished and more handsome than ever. She wasn't a complainer. Sure, she wanted him to go do things with her, and he was just clueing into the fact, it was his own fault he did not. He let the love in the marriage dwindle, not her. She indeed did everything she could think of to keep it from being mundane. When did he stop paying enough attention to her? When was the last time he sent her a big beautiful bouquet of flowers just because? They no longer went on picnics or any of the many things they used to do together.

PART IV - CHASTAIN

He was such a fool. The life he now had was not what he wanted. He wanted his wife, who had been more true to him than anyone in his life while putting up with him being gone all the time. Chastain…was this weight loss a direct issue from his leaving? Somehow, sometime, he had to talk to Donna. He would not blame her if she absolutely refused. After the cad he had been, why would she meet? He knew he had brought all of this on himself. He took the picture that had fallen and broke and threw it away. Even if Donna would not even speak to him, the chaos he was living had to go.

The following day, he broke the news to Rain that this was not working out and that she needed to pack. He was prepared for the barrage of tears that would come. Those had worked on him too long already. It was time for her to get out! He had called for a moving crew to load and haul her stuff wherever she wanted it taken. He had already begun packing some of her things the night before. He was almost giddy. This decision should never have even had to be made. He should have stayed home with the only woman he had ever really loved. He had actually prayed Donna would hear him out.

Donna had made the decision to go ahead and give the Bible Study a try. What could it hurt? If she did not like it, she did not have to go back. As it turned out, she was very profoundly touched at the study. A lady prayed with her and could not stop herself from crying. It was not about Robert this time. It was something deep within that she did not fully understand but wanted more of. After the prayer, she felt peace. A peace that passes all understanding. With the tumultuous life she had had; lately, it made no sense, but she basked in it. Maybe there really was something to all of this. She would definitely return. She wondered why she had been so harsh minded about it?

While Donna was gone, Rhett was left with Chastain. His repugnant actions simply made her feel sick. She repeated the same old things and then got to stay alone in her room. Why couldn't he find a job and get out? She hated him. He made her feel repulsive. He had undoubtedly ruined a love life for her when she got older. Marriage could just never happen now. Not with how she felt about herself and would never find a wonderful man if they knew about the real her. She loathed him and wished something terrible would happen to him. She

PART IV - CHASTAIN

certainly would not be saddened by it.

Robert waited several days before he called Donna. When she answered, she immediately told him to hold on, and she went to get Chastain. He interrupted her, saying he needed to talk to her. She very directly told him they had nothing to say to each other and hung up. She could just imagine what he wanted to talk about. The divorce. Or worse, what if he had decided he wanted to go ahead and marry Rain. Just the thought of her name was repulsive to Donna. The phone began ringing again, it was Robert. Donna told him not to call back unless he needed to talk to Chastain or Rhett and hung up again.

The following week at bible study, the lesson was on forgiveness. Donna started just to get up and leave. She would never forgive Robert for what he had done to her and their family. A woman gave a testimony about forgiving her husband and moving forward with their marriage after he had an affair. Donna gave thought to how hard that must have been. Then she thought, yeah, but he did not leave you for her. Her situation was totally different. As they neared the end of the lesson, her heart was very heavy. Forgiveness was not for the other person but for you. She would never have viewed it that way. Tears were formulating in her eyes. What in the world now? She did want freedom, but she just was not ready to give forgiveness yet. She discovered that deep within in heart, she kind of wished she could forgive him and start over. Like that would happen with Rain in the picture.

Again, Robert tried calling. He had come up with a new approach that he anticipated could open the door for more talk as well. Donna answered and straight away said that Chastain was at a chess lesson. Robert quickly told her the call was for her about Chastain. That made Donna change her mind. What about her she asked? Robert began talking to her in a loving manner, saying he knew she always did her best when it came to Chastain and her cherished that. But, asked if Donna had any idea how much weight Chastain had lost? This promptly got Donna's attention. You've noticed it too, she asked? He asked if they could meet and discuss it rather than over the phone. Donna was very timid about meeting him face to face. She was not sure she could handle it. Then it dawned on her, she was putting her own feelings above what was best for Chastain and now was not

PART IV - CHASTAIN

the time for that. They sat up a time to meet at a local coffee bar that had small booths where they could talk and be on neutral ground.

Chastain made it back home, excited about her lessons today. It was so good to see her smiling. She told her mom all about it. Donna was not a chess fan, but she listened intently. As she did, she was looking at how drawn Chastain's face had become. Her body seemed so frail. What was she not giving her that she needed, Donna wondered. Chastain had also received an application for the chess club. She knew she could not turn it in yet but just having it was thrilling to her. Donna did not tell her about the meeting with her dad.

Rhett had not been around in a couple of days, and the relief was felt throughout the whole house. Even the air permeated relief. Donna thought he might have found him a girlfriend and was staying with her. Whatever the situation was, she was glad about it.

The day had finally approached to meet with Robert. Donna did not know why, but she wanted to look her best. That was hard for her to feel after all that had happened. She no longer felt beautiful. She met him at the coffee shop dressed in a tan dress with white polka dots, tan pumps, and her pearls on that he had bought for her several years ago. She had her hair up in a twist. The moment she saw him, the air just sucked right out of her body. Knowing she was no longer attractive to him, why in the world had she tried to look pretty. Robert just stared at her. She was a vision to behold. He did think she looked beautiful but decided not to focus on her long delicate neck or her soft earlobes, which held her pearl earrings. He recognized the set he had bought her. Regardless of how self-conscious she felt, she asked to be seated. Robert ordered their coffee's for them. As he sat down, he was at a loss as to what to say. He needed to talk about Chastain but wanted to beg for forgiveness and get to come home. Donna cleared her throat and inquired what it was he had to say about their daughter.

PART IV - CHASTAIN

PART V
BIANCA

PART V - BIANCA

The next thing Bianca knew, Spring had arrived. School was great, and she loved that it got her away from home. The only difference in her relationship with Milo was that he moved the bed around so he could make her watch what was on the tv so they could practice what she saw. She really did not want to do what the girls on there were doing. She did notice that many of them looked near her age.

Milo and Leonard were starting their lawn care service back up. They had lost a few of the jobs from last year due to being late or not showing up to mow. They said they could make up for it this year.

Her mother had fallen at work and hurt her back. Milo was determined they would sue and get an excellent settlement. Annette was in bed most of the time, with pain pills and muscle relaxers. Milo would take alcohol in to her to help relieve the pain and relax her body better.

The nights in the basement continued. Bianca hated that sometimes her body would respond even though she did not want it to.

She and Natalee stayed connected throughout the summer. Their favorite part was going to the pool. Every time she came home though Milo would make her go down to the basement.

Annette had started feeling a bit better and was up and around with them a little more often. She was still taking the pills and drinking almost as much as Milo did.

Once again, it was time for school to start. First Milo dropped off Dana then Bianca. He was going back to get Annette to go see the attorney. They had bought a back brace the previous weekend, and her mother began complaining more about her back. After getting to school, she caught up to Natalee, who was hanging out with her brother and his friend. Bianca began to feel a little sick, but it passed by the end of the first hour. Natalee told her they needed to get together soon and have a personal conversation that would only be between them. They agreed with a pinkie swear and agreed to meet back up the next morning.

Bianca got to stay all night at Natalee's house that weekend. Bianca was shocked at what Natalee was telling her. It was apparent she liked Luke, and she said she had found out Luke liked her too. Her brother, Nathan, had told her and they had been meeting up a lot. Natalee told Bianca her brother thought she was cute and thought they could all get together

PART V - BIANCA

next time she came over. Bianca did not know what to think about a boy liking her. She nearly fell over when Natalee told her what they had been doing. She was fooling around with Luke. They weren't having sex, but she was letting him caress her, and her brother wanted to do the same with Bianca because he felt stupid just sitting around watching them. Bianca began feeling sick again. She complained of not feeling well and needing to go home.

    Bianca continued to feel sick for a couple of weeks. Her mother noticed and asked her if she had tried anything with the boys at school. Bianca vehemently defended herself. Of course, she had no! Milo was the only one, she did not say that out loud but was what she was thinking. Her mother pointed out she had noticed her and Milo had gotten pretty friendly while she was in bed in pain. Bianca did not consider it friendly necessarily. Her mother made her take a pregnancy test, and it was positive. Her mother demanded to know who the father was. Annette discussed it with Milo, and he told her about his encounters with Bianca. Annette could not believe they had not told her! She immediately made arrangements to take Bianca to have an abortion. She scolded Bianca, telling her that she should of let her know she was sexually active and she would have put her on the pill. Now they had a mess to take care of quietly.

Bianca had to miss a week and a half of school. Milo or her mother would go to school and get her homework. Her mother got the Dr to write a note so Bianca could miss school. Annette wanted to be sure Bianca was fine before sending her back to school.

When she returned, Natalee wanted to know what had been wrong. She called several times, but Bianca's mother would tell her Bianca was sleeping. The story was that she had the flu, and Bianca was never to reveal anything different. Natalee was excited to tell Bianca she was now Luke's girlfriend.

Bianca's grades began to fall. She did not really care about anything. Her father noticed she seemed much more withdrawn. When he would ask if she was okay, she always responded yes asking why he would ask that. He would assure her that he was just checking on her and making sure she was ok. He decided this was part of teenage hormones. He had big news for the girls. He had asked Angi to marry him, and she said yes. They wanted both girls to be in the wedding so it would be a family affair. They

PART V - Bianca

were having a Christmas wedding so the girls would be spending the week before Christmas with their dad, attend the wedding that Friday and then their dad and Angie would be off to their honeymoon.

There was shopping for the dresses and a couple of fittings to attend. Aunt Demi was involved and helped pick out their shoes and jewelry. She treated the girls and Angi to a day at the Spa and getting their nails done. Otherwise, the girls did not see much of their dad. He was so busy with work and had to get things in order for him to be gone on his honeymoon.

Annette was furious and yelled at Milo because they had not gotten married yet. A couple of weeks later, they took the girls to the courthouse with them, and the Justice of the Peace married them. They didn't go on a honeymoon. They simply returned home, opened a bottle of champagne, and went to the basement. Leonard came over later that evening to help them celebrate. Bianca was watching Dana for a day or two while they celebrated. If she needed anything, she was to open the basement door and yell for her mom but not to go down there after her.

Christmas came and went. While dad was on his honeymoon, Milo shared with Bianca that he had a special present for her for Christmas. She was actually thrilled to be getting a surprise that was all for her and not shared with her sister. She loved her sister, but it was nice for something to be only for her and a surprise at that. Her mother went through bouts of staying in bed, and other times she would be up and around taking it very easy but drinking heavily. They still had that dumb silver Christmas tree. Bianca had Dana help her, and they put it up and decorated it. Annette sat in the kitchen to oversee them making cookies. They were not the kind they got to make with Aunt Demi. It was a tube they cut pieces off of, but they did get to ice them.

Neither her mother or Milo were working. Things were very tight financially, but they did have assistance and food stamps. Annette kept saying it would all be much better after her court case. Bianca was sent down to the Dollar Tree to get a few gifts for her sister. She wanted to get some more decorations, but her mother told her they couldn't afford those kinds of luxuries and only to spend the money on 5 gifts for Dana.

PART V - Bianca

It was Christmas Eve, and Milo told her it was time for her surprise present. She just could not squelch the excitement she felt inside. A surprise when they had very little money! He told her it would not be long now and to go ahead and get showered. When she came out of the bathroom, Leonard was there. She hoped this did not mean her surprise would have to wait. She looked for her mom. She was passed out in bed. Dana was asleep. So much for the surprise. She simply felt defeated. Milo told her to come on into the living room. She said hello to Leonard, but it was pretty lame. Milo asked her if she was ready. What? There would still be a surprise even without mom? This was great! She was in complete shock when she found out Leonard was her surprise.

What did that even mean she wondered. Then everything turned horrifying. Leonard scooped her up over his shoulder, and Milo told her to keep her mouth shut! They took her to the basement. Of course, the tv was on. Milo did not think she would need it tonight but to make sure all went well made her sit and watch it for a bit. Then Leonard came over and started to remove her nightgown. She was in disbelief. She did not want this. This was not a surprise, this was a horror story. First, it was Leonard, then Milo. From there it went from bad to worse when she thought it could not possibly be any more unfavorable than it had already was.

PART V - BIANCA

PART V
SYBIL

PART V - Sybil

She and Samantha continued to find ways to meet the boys. Samantha met Allen more often than Sybil met Paul. Samantha and Allen had a full blown relationship. Sybil dreamed of being able to have one. Would that ever be possible? Would she ever have any solace and be somewhat normal? She wished she knew the answers. She was becoming more careless in her relationship with Paul. She wanted to be wanted. She wanted the attention of being worthwhile of being someone's girlfriend. She wanted people to see that she was lovable and desirable. Mainly she wanted it from someone closer to her own age. She no longer felt she ever knew what love really was. She had never actually seen love. She was growing up with anger, alcohol, beatings, belittling, and hearing how her dad HAD to marry her mom. Could there be love located in any of that?

The very people she trusted were not to be trusted. Why was she given to this family? Why was she put here to be humiliated? Why would God do this to her? Wasn't He the only one with the power to do so? She no longer went to church with her mom (who did not go very often anymore either) because she felt betrayed by God. Why did he let this happen? Why didn't he stop it? Why her? She had many more questions than she had answers.

Her cutting began getting a little deeper now. She needed more to drown out the pain each time her father assaulted her. She was so glad Samantha taught her this as a way to deal with pain. It was so much easier than trying to deal with her supposed family.

When she and Samantha would meet the boys, Samantha and Allen usually disappeared to be alone. One night she decided she would meet Paul with total abandon and do all the things he wanted. She wanted to experience all the things Samantha did. A guy that doted on her, called her beautiful, could not keep his hands off her, always greeting her with a kiss and always giving her a very long kiss goodbye. If she lived to regret it, she would just chalk it up to her worthlessness. Her desire was more than she could take these days. Right, wrong or indifferent, she wanted to know what it felt like to be loved even if only for a little while. She knew she wanted Paul to adore her for much more than just tonight, though. She needed that knight in shining armor to rescue her.

Sybil's dad would still do the same acts. All

PART V - SYBIL

she wanted was to be away from all of it. There was some type of rage beginning to bubble up inside of her. Sometimes she wondered why she thought of killing herself when it was her parents that should be killed. If only she could do that! The desire was real, the reality of it happening was not. Did she really want to spend her life in prison over them? The answer was no. Then the rest of her life would be ruined. Or would it? A part of her believed it would be worth it after all her dad had done to her and her mother allowing it. What was wrong with her mother, anyway? Why didn't she do anything? Why did she have to have freaks for parents? The things she had to do had just gotten worse over time… and her mother did nothing. She had caught him again. Again, Sybil felt blamed for it. She just wanted her mother to understand she did not want any of this to happen. However, she was not allowed to bring it up. She was the family's dirty little secret.

In High School, she and Samantha remained close but had begun to meet new friends as well. She and Paul had continued their relationship. Then, one day out of nowhere, he wanted to break up. Sybil was mortified. Why? What had she not done? What did she do wrong? How can she get him back? Questions were just swirling in her mind. One of the girls at school told her that Paul had been seeing another girl also. He was out of school now and had met someone else. Sybil felt totally shattered. She went home and got the knife for cutting to try and reduce this pain. She made several cuts this time and had quite a bit of blood smeared on the bathroom sink. Her mother walked in and was shocked at what she saw. She immediately took Sybil to the hospital. The wounds were not as bad as they looked, They bandaged both forearms and asked for a psych evaluation. She was admitted into treatment. In a way, she was relieved. Then she learned she had to go to group sessions and talk about herself. Yeah, right. That could not happen. She would only talk about her and Paul.

While in treatment, there was a guy she connected with. His name was Jesse, and he did not want to talk either. She would try to sit by him when she could. Weirdly he made her feel safe and like she was not crazy. She needed someone that could understand. She honestly felt like that someone was Jesse.

Amazingly enough, they were going to release her. She wanted to stay there where Jesse

PART V - SYBIL

was. She scribbled her phone number down for him before she left. This was so sad to her. What could she do to make people understand she needed him? It felt so unfair. She did not want to be there in the first place and then she met Jesse and did not want to leave without him. She was released with the treatment plan of following up with a therapist.

Needless to say, Samantha wanted all the details. She could not believe Sybil met a guy there! Samantha had broken up with Allen for an older guy. He had a job, his own place, and treated her well. She thought they might get married one day.

Upon her return home, her mother could not stop crying. She kept asking Sybil what in the world was wrong with her? Why would she do that? Had she even thought about the scars it would leave? Or how it would make her mom and dad feel. Sybil simply had nothing to say. What was wrong with her - she wanted to scream at the top of her lungs because she was being sexually abused! Why do it - to kill the pain, hate, and disgust for herself. Scars - no, she hadn't thought about scars, she was too busy killing the pain! How it would make them feel - are you serious? They have not been concerned one iota with how they made her feel, so no, no she hadn't thought about that.

The last place Sybil wanted to come back to was home. It was her own fault for not telling the truth about why she really cut herself. This was way too personal. The silence of the secret was deafening at the same time. Her entire world was nothing more than raging hurt, no self-worth, pain, distrust, and disgust. She wanted to scrub herself with a wire brush, but even that wouldn't make her clean!

Mason came over to see her. Oh, how she wanted to tell him! She knew if she did, Mason would probably kill their dad, and his life would be wasted in prison. He did not like his father or to be associated with him, to begin with. When he asked her why, she began to cry and lied. Her life was all lies. She simply said they were hoping a therapist could help her get to the bottom of it. He hugged her tightly, and they both cried. He reiterated several times to call him if she needed anything at all.

William called shortly after Mason left. He was extremely worried about his baby sister. Sybil could not burden him with the truth. He had a family and career to be concerned with.

PART V - Sybil

Their conversation was much the same as the one she had with Mason, without the hug. He did tell her, she was always welcome to come and stay with him and Gayla if that would help at all.

She knew her brothers had always loved her deeply and would do anything for her. This was the one thing they couldn't protect her from. The damage was already done. Athena had told both boys that Sybil was just acting stupid because she and her boyfriend had broken up. Both boys believed there had to be more to it than that. They absolutely couldn't fathom any of this.

Sybil returned to school. It did give her some comfort being around her friends again. They were the only thing she had really missed. She knew that was not entirely true. She did miss Paul. What she would give for a huge hug from him. Needless to say, the word at school was Sybil had been put in a psych ward for trying to kill herself when Paul broke up with her. There was not even an ounce of truth to it, but it was better than the real reason. She simply shared she had tried cutting, her life was never in danger, and she had to see a therapist to figure out why.

Several weeks passed, and Sybil happened to answer the phone. A voice she was unfamiliar with called her by name and asked how she was doing. It turned out, it was Jesse. He had not forgotten about her after all! She was elated to hear from him! He wanted to see her. They made plans to meet in the food court at the mall.

He was even more handsome than she remembered. Probably due to the way you look in treatment. You're not exactly at your finest. He had a new hair cut. His hair was black, eyes of blue and kept himself in shape. Turned out, he was 6 years older, but Sybil didn't care. She was anxious to start this new journey with him. He wanted to take her on a date. She almost squealed in excitement at the offer. Of course, she would. They made plans, and he would pick her up at 6:30 sharp next Saturday. They talked on the phone every night.

Sybil's mother was more than disappointed in her choice to already start dating. Athena still blamed the cutting on her previous breakup. Sybil couldn't decide if her mom was just that oblivious or genuinely believed she had no part in all that had happened. Sybil stood her ground and kept her plans. She and her mother

PART V - SYBIL

were both stunned when Jesse pulled up on a motorcycle! Sybil had never ridden on one, and the thought was very enticing. Jesse was very congenial with her parents and promised to take good care of her. He gave Sybil her helmet and off they went.

Jesse had been fired from his previous job due to his stint in rehab. Sybil thought that was completely unfair. They went to a nice restaurant with white linen table cloths. They talked nonstop. Sybil asked why he was in the ward. He was very open and specific that he had nearly ruined his life with alcohol. His job had already been in danger before the stay. He was in the yard, half dressed, yelling and carrying on. Neighbors thought he was on drugs and called the police. When he did the breathalyzer, it topped out, and they couldn't believe that could be correct and took him to the hospital for possible alcohol poisoning. They had to sedate him to get him calmed down, eventually admitting him to the psych ward. He told of how he had gotten involved with a rougher crowd in high school and had begun drinking his first year in. He asked if she would like to talk about what had happened to her. She simply told him that he had pretty much heard it in the group. He had to admit, it was rather unsettling to go out with someone that tried to take their own life over a breakup. She interrupted him to explain, she had indeed gone through a breakup and had tried cutting but never tried to take her own life. She got a bit indignant about it, telling him if he thought she was going to attempt suicide if he started dating her and they broke up, he was entirely wrong. He reached over and caressed her hand and apologized for upsetting her. She had to pull herself together. She had definitely become a bit irrational, and she apologized. All was good, and they left for the movie. The ride home on the motorcycle was nothing short of exhilarating. Sybil felt so free riding on the bike, wind blowing and her arms wrapped around Jesse. She hoped he had enjoyed himself tonight and would ask her out again soon.

    She was on cloud nine telling Samantha about Jesse and the difference in dating a man rather than a high school boy. Samantha couldn't help but laugh. She had been trying to explain that to Sybil to no avail! Then things became more serious as Samantha shared she was afraid she might be pregnant. Sybil was at a loss. What would her parents say or do? Would they throw her out the way her dad had thrown

PART V - Sybil

William out? Sybil was obviously flustered with this news. Samantha assured her everything was fine. If she were pregnant, she and Allen planned to get married; therefore, everyone would be happy. If she wasn't, they planned to marry anyway, so all was good.

Sybil had noticed she had a hard time concentrating on things and keeping her train of thought. Although it disturbed her, it would give her something to talk about with her therapist. Those appointments seemed to last forever, considering she didn't have much to say. She did finally explain she only tried self-harm because someone had shown it to her and she was very curious. She had to have something to say. Her dad was already mad; he was having to pay part of the bill.

PART V
CHASTAIN

PART V - Chastain

Robert discussed how frail and tiny Chastain was looking. Donna agreed and had no idea why their daughter had seemed to have become obsessed with weight. Robert told her about a gentleman he worked with whose daughter had an eating disorder. It could begin due to stress and/or trauma. He did not claim to understand it all. He just thought Chastain may need to go into treatment or something. Donna agreed. She would make a Dr. appointment for Chastain and address the issues. It would also tell her the child's weight. Maybe there was something other than treatment that could be done.

Robert could not help himself. Donna had her hands clasped, and he reached over with one hand and placed it over hers. Her hands seemed so small compared to his. For a few moments, all he could think of were the vows they had made years ago. Donna removed his hand and told him she would do her part. She was feeling a little sassy and said 'I'm sure you need to get home to Rain and I need to go back and read up about eating disorders and see if I think this may refer to Chastain. With that, Donna stood, turned on her heel, and walked away. Robert was so frustrated. Tears were beginning to well up in his eyes. He reminded himself that at least this was a step and he would tell Donna about kicking Rain out. He wanted to have done it today but knew he would become a blubbering mess begging to come back home. She was nowhere ready for that. Who knew if she ever would be. He just had to be thankful for today.

Donna went home and began reading up on eating disorders. She did not really feel this applied to Chastain. Nonetheless, she called and made a Dr. appointment. She asked if the Dr could please give her a call at his convenience about the need for the appointment so she would not have to go into all of it in front of Chastain. When he returned her call, he agreed it was too soon to be trying to diagnose anyone. He planned to do a complete physical and would rely on his findings, if any.

Chastain was not happy on the way to the appointment. She felt betrayed that she would have to go. She was not even sick. The Dr did his examination and spoke with Donna when he was done. He agreed something was definitely wrong and felt they needed to send her to a therapy center to get to the bottom of it. Her lab work was not normal. He felt she was not being honest with him about her weight

PART V - Chastain

loss, and they needed intervention. He had seen girls go through this before and it could get gruesome. He was going to make some calls to see where would be the best place for her. Nothing long term, she hadn't reached that point, yet. He told Donna he was going to speak with Chastain and let her know he needed to send her somewhere to see what was up with her lab work being so off and for her to see a therapist while there. For now, they were to go home and pack some things. He would call when he found the right place. He was going to check with a couple of other physicians for referrals as well. He planned to get her right in and hoped he could.

Donna called Robert while the Dr. spoke with Chastain. She simply gave him a quick heads up of what was going on.

When the girls arrived home, Robert was sitting on the porch waiting for them. Chastain was furious with her mother. She stomped into the house, slamming the door. Robert gave Donna a short empathetic hug and said he would talk to Chastain if she were alright with it. She willingly agreed, and he went to Chastain's room and asked if he could come in. He could see the fury in her eyes. She was raising her voice and accusing her mom of doing this to get rid of her. He finally got her to settle down a bit, and she crumpled into his arms in tears. Once she stopped sobbing, he let her know that it was not just her mom. He was responsible as well. He reprimanded her for saying either of them would want to get rid of her. They wanted her healthy. That was the reason for the physical. She began to cry again as she got up and grabbed a small travel bag.

Waiting for the Dr. to call seemed like an eternity. Chastain asked if her dad could stay and eat supper with them. This did not sit well with Donna. Donna looked around rather sheepishly at first then asked if he needed to call Rain and let her know. Robert instantly flashed mad. He let Donna know, in no uncertain terms, that when it came to the well being of their daughter, NO ONE had a say in what he would do. Tempers had flared momentarily. Robert was so mad at himself. He was the only one to blame, and he had let it get to him. He apologized to Donna saying they all just needed to settle down and enjoy this time right now. The phone rang, and Donna jumped. Chastain just stared at the floor, and Robert was right next to Donna, trying to hear what was being said. When Donna hung

PART V - Chastain

up, she let them know they had a place to go, and they were waiting for them. Robert drove. Donna and Chastain were both tearful during the ride. This was the most miserable trip ever. When they arrived, they got Chastain admitted and said their goodbyes. On the way back to Donna's, she would occasionally let out a sniffle and wipe her eyes. Otherwise, she was just quiet. A deafening sort of silence filled the car.

When they arrived at Donna's, they sat in the car for a few minutes. Donna wanted to scream at him. She was convinced this was all his fault for running out and sowing his wild oats. She hoped it was worth it to him. Her daughter meant everything to her. Robert was thinking of staying the night to help console Donna. He was the one that finally broke the silence. He asked if she would like him to stay. Just be there for her. He knew it would be harder on Donna than on him. She was used to being with her every single day. Donna looked at him as though he were a madman. Surely he was kidding. She hoped he swallowed his tongue for even mentioning it. She abruptly sent him on his way. She did not look back as she sprinted for the house.

She went to Bible Study, but this time, she actually shared a little about herself. Then the deluge of tears came. The women were very loving to her and gave her time to calm down. She told them about her daughter. They immediately began praying for her precious daughter, her and Robert as they went through this trying time. Then a pretty quiet lady usually, began to pray for her marriage. Donna was not sure how she felt about that! Had the women not heard her say he left? This prayer was tougher than the forgiveness lesson. She always felt heavy-hearted toward the bible study but always felt so much better at the conclusion of the night after she was prayed for. One of the ladies came to her and asked if she had received Christ into her life. She was not actually sure. So they said the sinner's prayer and the lady was sweet enough to explain how the devil would not like that and would try to make her miserable at every opportunity so at every chance she needed to pray. Donna's first thought was maybe she did really accept him already, and that's why she was going through this whole thing with Chastain now. Then it dawned on her the lady told her to pray. Wait. What? She had people pray for her, how was she going to do it? She

PART V - CHASTAIN

wasn't as spiritual as them. She hadn't always walked this life. What would she say? How do you do it? She had so many questions. It was related to her to say anything she wanted. God already knew how she was feeling, and He wanted to be there for her. One of the ladies pulled a book of prayers for every situation off the bookshelf and gave it to her.

She went home with her new book and began to peruse through the pages. It seemed this book really did have a prayer for everything. Then she saw it…prayers for your marriage. Wouldn't it be ludicrous to pray for that? Yet she felt drawn to it. She went through the pages and found a prayer for sickness, so she read that prayer for Chastain a couple of times, which made her cry. Before she knew it she was back to the pages of prayer for marriages. She couldn't help herself. She found herself praying these prayers. She wanted Robert back. She wanted him to come to his senses and come home. She was in disbelief she was admitting that to herself. She felt a tinge of hopefulness but told herself not to get too carried away or start expecting too much, especially too soon.

After a few days, the center called about Chastain. They wanted to set up a meeting with Donna and Robert. Some things had been discovered they should know. Donna hung up, immediately calling Robert to see when he could be available. He told her to set up whatever time they had, and he would make it happen. She heard the urgency in his voice. The same urgency she felt. She returned the call and set it up for 10am in the morning. Upon calling Robert back, he wanted to know if they said what was going on. They had not. He asked if Donna needed him to come over. She pondered the thought for a moment. She made it clear he could come over, and if he stayed, he would sleep on the couch. Period. He showed up with a bottle of wine. They ordered dinner in. The elephant in the room (which was Rain) was not brought up at all. After dinner, they had a glass of wine and reminisced about Chastain as she had grown up. They laughed at times, cried at others, and sometimes laughed until they had tears as they talked about her cute little antics growing up. At the end of the evening, Donna got Robert a sheet, blanket, and pillow for the couch. They said goodnight & Robert asked for a hug. Just the kind of hug that means everything is going to be alright, nothing more. No improper intentions.

PART V - CHASTAIN

As Donna lay in bed thinking about Robert in the other room, she kind of felt bad. She could have let him sleep in one of the additional bedrooms. She just felt that was almost too intimate. She wanted him home. This was not exactly what she had thought of, but there was something soothing about having in the same place as her.

The next morning neither of them had an appetite. Robert asked where Rhett was. Donna let him know he had been in and out but gone quite a bit, thinking maybe it was a girlfriend. Robert laughed and said let her have him! It will reduce the food bill! Donna chuckled. What she would give for Rhett to leave.

They arrived at the clinic and were asked to wait a few moments. Inexorably a lady came and invited them into her office. She shared that what she had to say was going to be very hard to take. It had really taken a toll on Chastain, and they had given her a sedative to help her sleep last night. Robert and Donna's interest instantly became a burden. Oddly enough, more so than when they brought Chastain in. The atmosphere completely changed. There was a sense of foreboding in the room. The tension became thick as they braced themselves to hear this news. They both thought they already knew what it was and Chastain was going to need long term treatment. Nothing could have been further from that as this lady began to speak. She asked them about Rhett. She wanted to know how long he had lived there, if he was home now, why he was living with them, etc. Donna clarified that Rhett was Chastain's uncle, noting it was the father's brother. Why was she so interested in Rhett?

PART V - CHASTAIN

PART VI
BIANCA

PART VI - Bianca

Christmas morning came, and Dana was up like a shot ready to see what Santa had brought. Bianca didn't even want to go out of her room. She was humiliated and felt dirty. What she really wanted was some control over something….anything…just something she even minutely had control over. She hated herself. She hated her life. At this point, she blamed her father. This was all his fault. If he had not driven her mother away, they would have a completely different life. Or would she? She was so perplexed she didn't know what to think. The one thing she did believe was that she wished they had never met Milo. She did her best to make it through the day. She received a few small gifts from the Dollar Tree as well. Mom and Milo bought each other bottles of liquor.

There were many more nights of Leonard coming over. This isn't how it was supposed to be. She did not actually know how it was supposed to be, but she did not think it was this.

Her mom went to court and did get a settlement, but it would be a while before she would receive it. In the meantime, money was terribly tight. Bianca did not eat at school because she did not want the other kids to know she got free lunches. It was not much, but it was some little something she could control. At this point, that was all she wanted.

Milo and Leonard were always talking about ways to make money. Bianca wanted to scream how about get a real job? The two of them were scheming up a plan. Bianca went outside and waited for Natalee. Nathan was bringing her to pick up Bianca who was getting to spend the day at Natalee's. She had made Natalee promise no boys, just the two of them.

The girls had a great day together, and Bianca wound up getting to stay the night. Nathan and Luke were there for a while. They all went out back to smoke. Bianca was not sure why she had not tried it before. She felt so relaxed. All the anxiety, hate for herself, disgust, and blaming herself all just sort of faded away. This was how she wanted to feel all the time. Natalee talked about Luke some, but for the most part, they kept their conversations away from boys. Bianca shared about her life not being what she had thought it would be like and how she did not really care for Milo, but her mom was married to him. She kept her secrets to herself. Unsure of how even her best friend would feel or what she would think, she did not

PART VI - Bianca

feel safe sharing any of it. So she only shared that she didn't like Milo because he never had a job, sat at home watching tv and drinking all the time. She was trying to describe how tough it was to live with him and how eerie he seemed without giving herself away. Natalee told her some Valium would help take care of that. Natalee's mom had some in the bathroom, and she ran and got a few. Giving them to Bianca telling her it would help with the feelings. They grabbed a beer from the refrigerator to wash them down. Bianca had extra to take home with her for extremely stressful times.

    The following weekend Dana and Bianca got to go see their dad and Angi. It was so nice to be away from home so much lately. But the weekend had a surprise mixed in it. Her dad and Angi sat both girls down and told them they were going to have a baby. Bianca was not happy like her father thought she would be. She just sat there looking at them, and then the tears began to fall. Damien was at a loss. Angi went and sat next to Bianca and hugged her for a few moments before asking what was wrong. Dana, on the other hand, was excited she would get a little brother or sister and wanted to start getting ready. Angi took Dana in the kitchen for a drink and to talk about the baby. Damien wanted to know what was wrong with Bianca. With tears in her eyes, she told him another baby was not something she thought he would want. As it was, he barely had time to see her and Dana. Now they would never see him because he would be too busy with his new kid. She was accusatory, not inquiring. She told him that she had always thought someday he would miss his kids and come get them. Bring them back home where they belonged. Instead, he just gets a new one after he had told the girls no one could ever take their place yet, here he was, replacing them anyway. He hugged her and tried to explain it was not that way at all. He tried to express how important both of them were to him. Bianca did not believe him. She only believed that she could not trust anyone. She wondered if this was Angi's plan all along. For the first time, Bianca was glad to get to go back to her mom's after a weekend with her dad. Once she got back home, she took one of the valiums, called Natalee and asked what if she needed more. Natalee allowed her mom always had a bunch of them, and they could get more anytime.

Finally, school was out for summer. Kids

PART VI - BIANCA

had begun to make fun of her, calling her a loser with no money. They were right. Her clothes usually came from a thrift store and didn't always fit very good. She didn't eat lunch at school so the kids wouldn't know she got free lunches. Neither her mom nor stepdad had or would keep a job. Her mom's settlement was supposed to be coming, but she didn't believe they could live on it for very long.

The plan Milo and Leonard came up with this time to make money was the usual mowing and something extra special. Milo was very secretive about it and said he wasn't going to sell drugs or anything and if he was bringing money in, what difference did it make? Annette just agreed to whatever he wanted to do.

Natalee stayed all night with Bianca once school was out. It was a welcome fun night. Natalee brought Valium with her so Bianca would have a stash of it. Bianca's mom & Milo were in the basement, so they pretty much had the house to themselves once Dana went to bed. There was some Tequila left in a bottle, so they did a couple shots of it. Bianca loved the way the Tequila and Valium made her feel. Usually, it was Vodka, but they decided to try something different that night.

Bianca was starting to act out, and her mother was very frustrated with her. Annette kept threatening to send her to a girls home if her behavior did not improve. She and Natalee had begun sneaking out at night and hanging out with the older boys. Bianca had started to like Nathan, which made Natalee happy because she liked Luke. They would be out drinking at night and back home in bed by morning, occasionally with a hangover. Bianca's mom grounded her to stop the nonsense. Great, now she just had to be at the house with her mom and Milo. At least Dana was there, and she could play with her.

One night Milo had some friends over. Annette went to bed early. Once Dana was in bed, Bianca just stayed in her room. She needed a drink but knew it could not be alcohol with all the men in there. One of the men were in the kitchen and leaned into her and said, someday I want to own you all for myself. The men were getting rather loud and rowdy. Of course, Leonard was there. She heard him shushing everyone so they could talk about why they were really there. Later on, Milo came and got her, taking her to the basement. She wished she would have taken a Valium earlier. He told

PART VI - BIANCA

her it was time to unveil his other business for making money. It was then Bianca realized, not only was Leonard there but so were 3 of the other men. Bianca was scared out of her wits as to what may be about to happen. She began crying, and Milo grabbed her by her hair and yanked her to the side. He asked her if she wanted to see herself and her sister not having clothes that fit? Or maybe she wanted him to start in with Dana. He demanded answers from her. Her crying stopped. It had never dawned on her that he may do this to Dana one day. She had to protect her and keep her safe from all of this.

To bring in extra money, Milo decided to share Bianca. It was the most horrible thing yet. Never did Bianca fathom this would happen. Everything else had been bad enough, and now these men were going to be allowed to take turns. Bianca kept wondering how she would survive this and most of all, how to protect Dana from it. She just could not help but to let a tear slip out sporadically. When it was over, she went upstairs, grabbed a half-full bottle of Vodka, and polished it off. The degradation, humiliation….she couldn't help but wonder what she had done to deserve all of this.

Her mother began accusing her of taking alcohol from the house. She had been. She could not stand her life. It was drink and numb it or take her own life. She could not take her own life because that made Dana free game in this kaleidoscope of chaos. Her mom referred to her as rebellious snot that needed a good girls home to straighten her out. She could not get past the thought of Dana ever being in danger of Milo. Very strong hate had begun overtaking her.

Bianca was so glad when school started back up. Even if the kids made fun of her, it had to be better than being at home. The torture and torment were more than she could handle anymore. She would take Valium every day and preferred it with alcohol, but that was harder to do when in school.

Natalee was very concerned about her. She felt more was going on than she knew about. One weekend she asked Bianca to stay all night. Her parents would be gone, and it would be a great girl time. Natalee never saw the bomb coming that Bianca dropped on her that night. She didn't tell the whole story, just the part about Milo and what he'd been doing to her. They cried together, and Natalee had a better

PART VI - Bianca

understanding of all the valium and alcohol. She didn't know what to do. How do you help your friend in a situation like this, especially after you promised it would be a secret. Natalee wanted to kill him for doing what he had to her friend.

A few weeks later, Bianca was called to the office. The school counselor wanted to see her. As gently as the counselor could, she let Bianca know that she knew everything and was there to help her. Bianca finally broke down and told her about Milo. Child Welfare Services were called and came to pick her up. She had to retell her story again. In a way, she resented Natalee for telling and in a way she was relieved. She was being told what would happen now. She was so scared. She knew this was all her fault, and now she was going to make it worse. Child Welfare Services also picked up Dana. They were placed in a foster home together.

Having to retell what had happened was grueling. She just wanted it to be over with. Charges were filed against Milo and a court date set. While in foster care, it was discovered she had a drug and drinking problem. The plan was to send her to get cleaned up.

The trial was even worse than she anticipated. Milo denied everything. He said she was a habitual liar who had had it in for him from day one. Then her mother took the stand. She lied. She even lied about taking her to get an abortion. She said Bianca had been a problem since she and Milo started their lives together. Always whining about every single thing Milo would do. Even when they were playing, Bianca would continuously find things to complain about. She blatantly protected Milo and called Bianca a liar. The court ruled in their favor and sentenced her to a nearby girls home for her drinking and drugs. Dana was released back to the family. This caused uncontrollable anxiety for Bianca.

She suffered from nightmares, guilt, startle reflex, mistrust, insomnia, and poor self-esteem. Once she was released from treatment, she went back into the system. She would act out in many different ways. She just wanted her valium and alcohol back, she could not bear the pain and hurt. She was moved from three foster homes due to her inability to go by the rules and be respectful. She could not be respectful when there was a man in the house she did not know and was not aware of what he might be

PART VI - Bianca

capable of. The last family she stayed with did begin to give her a bit of a sense of security. The husband kept a healthy distance, which helped tremendously.

Eventually graduating, she aged out of the system. She went to Natalee's house. Nat's mom agreed to her staying with them, but she would have to find a job or be going to college or tech classes. Bianca happily agreed. She got a part-time job waiting tables and began taking classes at the Vo-Tech. She wanted to be a secretary and needed more skills. Along the way, she had appalling memories that still haunted her. They not only haunted her, they caused great distress. She had no idea what love was or how to trust anyone after what had happened to her. She did not interact much with the other students. She was afraid they might know her from the court case or something.

Then there was this one boy. He was so handsome and so charming to her. He spoke softly to her, didn't make a lot of sudden movements and never tried to touch her. He asked her out after class, and they went for coffee. She had a wonderful time and hoped he asked again soon. His name was Tucker, and he was considerably taller than her, making her feel protected. He had sandy colored hair and hazel eyes. His eyelashes were soo long. She was slightly baffled as to why he would take her out for coffee but was ecstatic that he did. Soon going out to coffee turned into a dinner and movie date. Natalee helped her get ready. They were so excited.

PART VI - Bianca

PART VI
SYBIL

PART VI - Sybil

Her father had stayed away from her. No more wrestling or roughhousing. It was such a huge relief to her. There was a difference in relief and forgiveness, and she had no plans to ever to forgive him or her mother.

Somehow, her mother had found out Jesse was six years older and had his own apartment. She forbid Sybil ever to see him again. They were having a huge fight over it when her dad came in. He wanted to know what was going on. Once Athena had told him what she had found out about Jesse, he was mad also. Now they were both yelling at her. Her father pointed out that Jesse was up to no good. He was only after one thing, and James refused to have another child get pregnant out of wedlock. Sybil could not believe what she was hearing. All things considered, she did not believe they should have any say so about this. They told her due to her defiance and terrible attitude to go to her room. She marched away gladly. She would not tolerate this. She would run off first. She would leave school and get a job. She would stay with Mason for a while if she had to.

After everyone had gone to bed, she went into the living room and called Jesse. She told him the whole story. She could not help but cry while she talked. She knew they had not known each other very long, but she could swear her feelings were actually that of love. She had not felt this even when she was with Paul. Jesse reassured her, so she calmed down some. He told her not to worry, he would think of something. If appealing to her parents didn't work, he would come up with a new plan. She tried to settle down but wound up crying herself to sleep.

    The following evening, Jesse came by to speak with Sybil's parents. It got him nowhere. Other than her dad threatening to throw him out the door, it was a wasted trip. Although that part was a bit comical. Jesse went ahead and left. Sybil was in tears again and threatened to go live with Mason. That really set her dad off. Sybil just wanted to finish school and get out of there. Now she understood why William and Mason had felt.

    The following day just dragged by. All Sybil wanted was to talk to Jesse. She just hoped he would still speak to her. Things had gotten really ugly between him and her parents. They had no right to speak to him the way they did much less threaten to throw him out the door. She truly felt Jesse had handled himself as a

PART VI - Sybil

gentleman. Just the fact he came to try and talk civilly with her parents spoke volumes to her.

She went to Samantha's after school so she could call Jesse. She would wait and not call him at work. She did not want to get him in trouble with his new boss. She called him as soon as she could. He spoke very soothingly and told her not to worry. He would come up with a plan. They made plans to meet at the mall that weekend, and he would pick her up. He promised he would have a proposition by then. She told Samantha what had happened and how gallant Jesse seemed to come to her rescue while refusing to stop seeing her. Samantha had good news. She wasn't pregnant after all. She and Allen had told her parents of their plan to marry, and they were agreeable. It was not going to happen until after she graduated, however, Allen was going to pick out a ring for her. Sybil was overjoyed for her. Then Samantha asked her to be her maid of honor when they did get married. She had bridal books and some ideas written down that she shared. Sybil was not sure how to feel. She wanted what Samantha was getting but wasn't jealous. She was still heartbroken about Jesse but excited at the same time for Samantha and Allen.

When Sybil arrived home, her parents accused her of being with Jesse. She was so relieved she had a copy of Samantha's plans for her wedding. They clarified that Jesse better not come by. Her dad was saying he couldn't be held responsible for what he would do to that boy. Sybil just turned on her heel and went to her room. She refused to listen to her dad, belittle Jesse. Her dad continued to yell obscenities about Jesse even after her door was shut. This was going to be a long evening. She found that thought a bit humorous when she thought about how long it would be before she saw Jesse again. That was going to seem like an eternity.

Saturday finally rolled around. She could not wait to go to the mall. Jesse arrived, and Sybil got on the motorcycle. He took her out by a pond to talk where it was quiet and relaxed. It had a small dock on one side, and that was where they sat with their legs dangling just above the water. Sybil immediately began apologizing again, and Jesse shushed her and held her head to his shoulder. He told her that none of it had been her fault. In a way, he expected it or something like it to happen. He wanted to clarify her age. She thought it was such an odd request.

PART VI - Sybil

She was already 18 but hadn't graduated yet due to her birthday and starting school later than most. She was surprised because this was information he already knew. He presumed she already knew what was coming. He pulled a ring out of his pocket and asked her to marry him. The sooner, the better so all of this would be behind them. Sybil was speechless at first. Then she exclaimed yes. Her dream was coming true much sooner than she had imagined. Then she just kind of deflated. She looked down at the water and asked when he was thinking of doing this. Her parents would never agree. He laughed. She was beside herself! She was being completely serious, and he laughed at her. She looked at him wide-eyed as though he had lost his mind. As sweetly as he could, he told her that was why he asked about her age first. With her already being eighteen, she could go ahead and get married without parental consent. He wanted to go off and get married, they would live in his apartment, and he would ensure she finished school. She threw her arms around his neck. He had thought of everything. But wait… her dad would never allow her to have her things, not even her clothes. Jesse had thought of that also and had checked to be sure the authorities could go with them to get personal belongings. He indeed had thought of everything.

Sybil wanted to call Samantha, but Jesse would not let her. He thought they need to keep it between themselves until it happened to ensure her safety when it came to her dad's temper. Since they were running off to get married, Samantha would not be there. As lovingly as he could he let her know that one day they would have a real wedding but for now he could not live without her. He kissed her, then grabbed her by her shoulder and asked if she was ready for the details of their wedding. She was in awe of how much thought he had put into all of this. She shrugged her shoulders, squealed of course and hugged his neck. She didn't want ever to let go. Then she heard him say Monday. This was the most bizarre thing. She pulled back gazing at him and said, Monday what? He laughed. You silly girl, instead of going to school I'll pick you up there and you will become my Mrs. I believed you would say yes so I found a little chapel where you can get your blood work done while you get your marriage license and when it's ready, they walk across the street and get married. You'll have a bouquet and candles surrounding us. On the one hand,

PART VI - Sybil

she wished she had a real wedding dress, but she had a white dress that would suffice.

When he picked her up at school Monday, he was driving a sleek, black sedan. It was gorgeous. He had to step out of the car for her to realize it was him. She ran to him, gave him a hug, and asked where he got the car. He let her know she didn't know everything about him yet and to get in. He opened the door for her, and she got in. Off they went, to go to their little chapel. She did not even know where it was, nor did she care, she was with Jesse, and all was right in the world.

They drove for a couple of hours, and Jesse announced they had arrived. The town was more prominent than she had imagined it would be. She pictured a small, quiet, lazy town. They ran up the stairs of the courthouse, but before they went in, Jesse stopped her and placed her engagement ring back on her finger where it belonged. The wait for the blood test took longer than she expected, and she was growing impatient. Finally, the time had arrived to go across the street to the wedding chapel. It was absolutely beautiful. Sybil was not sure what she had expected, but it was not this. Everything from the moment you walked in was a wedding. And today, it was her wedding. There were beautiful heart shaped candelabras with candles just like Jesse had said. A lady took her to a room to pick out her perfect bouquet. Jesse received a matching boutineer. Sybil was dressed in a white dress with an asymmetrical hem. It had a little white jacket that went with it and it was perfect for the day

.The lady helping her went out of the room to make sure everything was ready. When she came back, she led Sybil back down the hall. There was touling hanging from the door where she had looked into the chapel earlier, and she could see tiny lights down the aisle. She didn't remember those being there. The wedding march began to play, and Sybil's eyes filled with tears. Either this place was perfect, or Jesse had thought of everything, or both. The touling was pulled back to allow her to enter. Each pew had flowers and a bow that matched her bouquet. And the twinkling lights were hung from the ceiling. It was beautiful. Then she looked down the aisle. She was slightly confused as she saw Jesse standing there in a suit looking even more handsome than ever. They also thought to have a few people in the room! A gentleman stepped to her side and walked her down the aisle to

PART VI - SYBIL

Jesse. Her enthusiasm was mixed with tears she was trying to hold back so it wouldn't mess up her makeup. This was a fantasy come true! Jesse took her by the hand and escorted her to the pastor for their vows. This was the most romantic thing in the world. She did not need a 'real' wedding, this was her real wedding! Jesse kissed the bride, and the pastor introduced them as man and wife to the people gathered there.

Jesse had one more surprise for her. The people there in the pews...they were some of his family. She was taken aback by this news. Jesse snuggled her neck and told her a wedding wasn't complete without family. As he said it, a lady came up and hugged her. It turned out to be his mother. The gentleman that walked her down the aisle was his dad! It was a bit overwhelming, but it was perfect. She turned and looked into Jesse's eyes and told him she loved him, and he was perfect. All of this was much more than she had ever expected and made knowing they had to return to Charleston and face the wrath of her parents much more manageable.

His father stepped up and told her that he was going with them to get her stuff. He wanted a legal advisor there as well and the sheriff's department to make sure everything went smoothly. He hugged her saying this had all been too beautiful to spoil. He was also sending them on a honeymoon after they took care of her parents. They all traveled back to Charleston. Jesse's father, Gerard, and another man got into the car with them. He sent the others to Jesse's apartment..

PART VI - Sybil

PART VI
Chastain

PART VI - CHASTAIN

She explained that according to what they had been told, Rhett had been sexually abusing Chastain. Donna gasped, and Robert exclaimed, what? The tone of his voice was one Donna had never heard from him. He stood to his feet, and the lady asked him to please sit down. She realized this was very unnerving information, but she needed both of them to listen to her. They were required by law to notify authorities in such cases. Robert exclaimed when he was done, there would be no need for authorities! He was livid. He wanted to race out of the room right this minute, find Rhett and beat him to a pulp and then file charges against him. He wanted Rhett in prison. He wanted him to rot there. The administrator got him to calm down. She let them know there was an officer outside the office waiting for the family to be informed of the situation. They were going to arrest Rhett. That's why she wanted to know if he was at the home. But the most important thing at this moment was to know if it went to court, Chastain would have to testify. This would be very hard on her. The defense attorney would try to make it look like it was all her fault. Although she was young, it wouldn't stand, but it would take a toll on Chastain. Then Donna asked the inevitable question. Why didn't she tell us? She was afraid you wouldn't believe her. He has convinced her that she deserved everything she has received. Her own value and self-worth are at nothing. That's why all of this with the eating. She felt her life was out of control, and she needed something she had a say-so over. She felt it was the only thing she had control over in her life. That is a side effect of all she had been through. We will be working closely with you and Chastain to work all of this out. Right now, I want you to get to see your daughter and the police will go arrest Rhett.

When Chastain came in, she immediately began sobbing and apologizing. Both of her parents were telling her, it was not her fault. It was Rhett's. He was a sick man that was going to jail for what he had done. Chastain asked if he was back at the house? They were not sure. She asked if Rhett knew dad had been there? He was afraid of dad. The last time, she threatened to tell Robert and Rhett said he would kill them all if she did. Then he was not hardly coming around. Robert asked her why she had not gone ahead and told him. She said she knew they would not believe her and would blame her also. This made her daddy cry, as well. He would

PART VI - CHASTAIN

have believed her. He may have gone to jail over it, but he would have believed her.

They gave them a private room to talk. Chastain had become so upset again, she was given a mild sedative. The therapist had also asked what he had done to her. She told her parents, she didn't have words to describe the despicable things that went on. Her meltdown had come at the knowledge she could have to go to court and give a detailed description. Her father was holding her as she looked up and asked him if they would really do that to her. He hugged her tighter and told her he did not truthfully know be he hoped not also.

An officer stepped into the room, asking to speak with the father. They went back to the administrator's office to talk. They had found Rhett walking a few blocks from their house. They had searched his room and found child pornography and pictures that would ensure Chastain wouldn't have to testify in court. The officer was confident Rhett knew he did not have a chance with all of the evidence they had. He told Robert they were welcome to go home now. The administrator kept Robert for a few moments, explaining the type of help Chastain would need. Although she could get better, she was likely to have PTSD. She would probably live with some fear in her life, and she would have triggers. She explained what those were and then let him get back to his family. Her Dr. thought it would be best for her to be with her mom and dad now. Chastain would return weekly for an undetermined amount of time.

Robert went and got his wife and daughter to take them home. First, he assured Chastain that Rhett was in jail and could not get to her. When they arrived home, Chastain found a note in her room on the bedside table. It said 'I will still own you'. Chastain began screaming, and her parents ran to see what was wrong. They called the police and asked for an officer to come and get the note if it would help the case. Donna was consoling Chastain as Robert made the call. Afterward, they all went into the living room and snuggled up on the couch. Donna turned on the tv, and there was a picture of Rhett as someone from the news covered the story and charges filed. At first, Donna regretted it, but it seemed to help Chastain. Suddenly it was all different. By seeing him in handcuffs and the mug shots made her feel better. Now she knew where he was, and she was ok. She did not need to worry about him trying to kill anyone. She

PART VI - CHASTAIN

still would be afraid, because it would take a long time to get over, but this was a step forward. Robert stayed that night. Chastain was scared, and Donna was pretty unnerved herself. They all got into Donna's bed with Chastain in the middle to help her feel more secure. The treatment center had sent them home with mild sedatives for the daytime and something a bit stronger for nighttime.

Robert stayed with the girls for the next few days. One night after Chastain was asleep, Donna asked about him staying there. She softly said she was not trying to start a fight, was just curious how Rain was taking the situation. Robert was caught a little off guard. He sat silently for a few moments. Donna broke the silence by apologizing for asking, it was not any of her business. Robert looked at her for a long time before replying. He shared that there was a whole story behind that and he had wanted to talk to Donna about it, but it just had not been the right time. Donna told him to proceed, she did not have any plans for the rest of the evening.

Robert was not sure where or how to start. As much as he had wanted to talk to Donna, this caught him out in left field. He had rehearsed what he was going to say when and if he ever got the opportunity. Now he felt like he had a cotton ball stuck in his throat. He shut the television off and explained this was going to be very difficult for him. Asking her to please bear with him. All at once, he knew where to start. He told her that an apology could not change what had happened, but that is what he wanted to begin with. After his apology, he went on to share how he had realized Donna was everything he had ever wanted. How gut-wrenching it had been to realize he had chased some wild fantasy when in truth, had he done those same things for her, their love would not have dwindled. He explained how he could now see all the times Donna had tried to keep the spark in the marriage. How lonely she had become while he was gone so often. He shared the dawning moment of realization that had he paid more attention, offered more affection, made sure they went on fun vacations, sent flowers for no reason and made more time for her none of this would have happened. He took her for granted rather than taking care of her emotionally.

Donna sat there wide-eyed. She could not believe she was hearing this. Finally, Donna

PART VI - CHASTAIN

asked if he was just using the excuse to stay with her and Chastain to be away from Rain. He set off an a rant about Rain and how wrong he had been and the answer to her question was no. The truth be told, he had moved Rain out before he contacted Donna for the meeting about Chastain. He told her how he had wanted to meet and tell her all of this but was afraid, she would not listen. So, the problem Chastain was having seemed like the best place to start. He shared he had even prayed he would one day get this moment but did not honestly believe it would happen. Donna did not say a word. She had been on the verge of tears as he told her about his realization of all he had done wrong. Now she stood up and walked away. Robert thought to himself he had ruined it by saying everything at one time. In a few moments, she returned with a book. It was her book of prayers, and she shared what she had prayed over Chastain. Taking a deep breath, she told him about the prayers for their marriage, although she had not believed it could happen either. Then she showed him those prayers as well. They both broke down right there on the couch. He leaned over, putting his arms around her and telling her that he had never stopped loving her. How there were times, she was all he could think about. He did not want what he had, he wanted to be with who he loved. After many tears and hugs, it was time for bed. Donna went and got him the things for him to make up his bed on the couch. He thanked her profusely for letting him stay during this time.

PART VI - CHASTAIN

PART VII

BIANCA

PART VII - Bianca

Bianca graduated her classes. It so happened Tucker's dad owned a furniture store, and they needed a secretary. Tucker took her to meet his dad and fill out an application. They hired her on the spot. She was elated and dreamed of having her own place.

Her father would occasionally check on her. While she was going through foster care and treatment, he told her that he could not just take her home with him, he had his family to think of as well. She really felt she had no-one until Tucker. Tucker helped out at the furniture store while finishing his classes. They continued to go out. One night when he dropped her off, he asked if it was ok to kiss her. She was taken aback. She had never kissed a boy because she liked him. She agreed. The kiss was very pleasurable. He walked her to the door, kissed her again before leaving after making sure she got inside okay.

What Tucker didn't realize was Bianca had begun drinking vodka again. Not to the same extremes, but she kept a flask in her backpack for the times she felt overwhelmed. The nurse at the treatment center had explained why she should not drink with her medications, but it was like she just could not help it.

Her job was perfect. The way the desk was set up, no-one could randomly walk up behind her. She was so thankful for that because it was such a trigger for her.

Eventually, Dana wound up with her father. It became apparent Annette and Milo would never take proper care of her, so DHS had been called in and removed her from unlivable conditions. Bianca's mom had gotten her settlement, but they had blown it in a matter of months and were back to nothing.

When Tucker asked about her family, she only spoke of her father. She did tell him that her mother had left for another man that was no good. She did not dare share any details of what had happened to her. Tucker was a good guy and would never want to settle for a filthy, no good girl like her. Tucker graduated, and it was a grand celebration held at the store! Finger foods, snacks, cake, drinks (non-alcoholic) and fun. Bianca was so proud of him. Later, the two of them went down by the river. In the moonlight, Tucker pulled a box out of his pocket, apologized that the ring wasn't bigger but was all he could afford right now and proposed to her. Now, it really was the perfect night. Of course, she said yes!

PART VII - Bianca

It took a few months for Tucker to get his work exams done, get a job and get on his feet. In the meantime, they made plans for what they would like at their wedding but didn't set a date until all was settled. Also, they would like to have a bit bigger apartment than the one Bianca lived in. Tucker wanted to move her to a better neighborhood that was closer to their jobs. Still, Bianca continued to drink. Sometimes it was out of fear of getting married. Would she really be able to have a full married relationship with Tucker? As much as she wanted to, she was fearful.

Of course, Natalee was going to be her Maid of Honor. They were not planning an outlandish wedding by any means, but Bianca wanted Natalee with her. Bianca's dad was happy for her and told her to let him know an approximate cost so he could pay for it. She totally didn't expect that!

How do you actually love someone? This question kept returning. Would she know how to do it right? What if she did something to upset him? Many more reasons to need a sip from the flask. She loved Tucker and was not afraid of him any longer. She just needed him to be patient with her and hoped that was not too much to ask. She would never tell him about her childhood; therefore he did not know all of her underlying fears. She thought surely when you love someone this just all comes together.

They began apartment hunting and found the perfect place. They put down their deposit and Bianca moved in. Only 6 more weeks and Tucker would be there with her as her wonderful husband. The closer it got, the scarier it got for her. And the more she drank. At the same time, she could not imagine her life without Tucker. She would do whatever she had to. Tucker's dad was giving them a 10-day cruise for their honeymoon. She was packing for that as well. It was all so much fun. She frequently wondered after everything she had brought on herself as a girl, how did she deserve this sweet, precious, gentle, man?

Finally! The wedding day arrived. Everything was so beautiful. Bianca was euphoric that her dad would be walking her down the aisle with Angi, Dana and Damien Jr. present. She could not imagine this day being any better and looked forward to the cruise that would follow. During the reception, the guests were eating and dancing. During this fabulous time, a gentleman stepped up to her side and simply

PART VII - Bianca

said, 'one day I will still have you'. She couldn't believe the words she just heard. She turned to see one of Milo's friends standing there. Bianca became very discombobulated, not knowing what to say or do. She wanted to throw her drink in his face. Scream for him to leave. Why would he show up and ruin her wedding day? He had never participated in the shenanigans in the basement, but she vividly remembered him telling her that before. He said to her that her mom had wanted a couple pictures, and that was why he was there. As quickly as he had appeared at her side, he was gone. She needed an excuse, any reason at all to step away from the reception. She needed her flask. She needed a long stiff drink to relax her, and the champagne wasn't going to do that. She told Tucker she was going to step away to the ladies room and take her shoes off for a few minutes as well but would rejoin him soon. She slipped into the room where her things were and took a long draw off the flask. How was she going to enjoy her honeymoon now? How was she going to enjoy the rest of the reception and the flight? She decided to add a valium to help get her through. She rejoined Tucker quickly, and they continued the reception with no further interruptions. Soon, they were loading their bags to head out for their romantic honeymoon.

During the honeymoon, Tucker seemed distant at times. She wondered if he could tell she was used goods. She had drank rather heavy and fought hard not to think about any of the horrible things that had happened to her.

As time passed, Tucker noticed just how much she drank. They would get into arguments about it. After finding her stash of valium, he demanded to know what the pills were and where she was getting them! She tried to explain her anxiety to him. He kept wanting to know why she had so much anxiety. She could not tell him the truth. She just knew he would leave her. Her happily ever after did not seem as happy as she had expected. Tucker told her in no uncertain terms if she continued with the pills and alcohol she was going to treatment whether they could afford it or not. Which was exactly where she wound up.

The therapist at the treatment center tried to get her to confide in Tucker. She just could not do it. She would never let him know about the things she caused to happen to herself. Her disgust and animosity toward herself continued in a huge inner battle. She was in treatment

PART VII - Bianca

for three months. Her first round of many trips there.

Eventually, Tucker just could not take it anymore. Each trip back to treatment took a significant toll on him as well. He felt like a failure as a husband and had no idea what to do any longer to try and make Bianca happy. Nothing had worked up until this point, and this was the fourth time in as many years. He did not want to abandon her, but he certainly did not know how to handle her. It was not just drinking and the valium. Even in intimate times, she did not really partake. He felt like he was just taking advantage of her and she was just going through the motions but did not really want to. He had felt like he was a failure and could not please his wife since the very beginning of their honeymoon. She acted happy enough at times, but she had become very temperamental, wanting to stay in her room to watch tv and drink. He made an appointment with a marriage counselor. It was the only thing left to try.

When she returned home, she looked so much better and was happy. That was until Tucker told her about the fantastic marriage counselor he had found and how he could not wait for both of them to start going. She adamantly refused. She could not tell him, but she would never go to a counselor and be honest, so what would be the point. This created a massive gap in their relationship.

In treatment, they wanted her to go to Alcoholics Anonymous when she returned home. She was not about to go there. She did not want the stigma that went with that. She had met a lady, while in treatment that tried to tell them about Jesus and how he could heal them. She led a group of ladies that needed help moving forward from many different things. One thing she said that really stuck out to Bianca was the word "abuse". She actually referred to sexual abuse. Bianca had never really been to church and was not sure about all of this, and at the same time, there was something about that lady that wouldn't leave her mind. She wanted to save her marriage, so she decided to give the lady a call and go to their next gathering.

This really hurt Tucker. Bianca would not go to marriage counseling with him, but she would go to some kind of group only for women. Tucker continued with his counselor and Bianca attended the next gathering. She went to an open group. She did not know what to expect. She was so surprised. The women were

PART VII - Bianca

exceedingly welcoming. Everyone shared a little about themselves. They did not go into details, just what they were struggling with. When asked if Bianca would like to share anything she simply said she had been in treatment and wanted her marriage to be healthy and thriving. A young lady named Chastain was in the group. She spoke of having been in treatment herself and with the help of the group was realizing she needed assistance in overcoming the sexual abuse she sustained as a child. Bianca was stunned. Chastain had actually spoken of sexual abuse out loud. Bianca began to cry. There was just something about this place that made her so comfortable and needing more.

After the group was over, a handful of the girls were going for coffee, so Bianca joined them. She wanted to hear more about them, particularly Chastain. Bianca felt she was already forming relationships. Was that possible in only one evening? What was the presence of peace she could feel so strongly?

It was bound to happen, and one night it did. Bianca and Chastain were chatting, just the two of them. Chastain spoke of her sexual abuse as a child. Bianca broke down into tears. A dam had burst. For the first time as an adult, she told someone about a lot of her abuse. She left some out because she just was not ready to share the depth of it. Chastain spoke to her about Jesus. His love, sacrifice, healing, and peace. Bianca accepted Christ into her life that night.

Eventually, Bianca went to the group for sexually abused girls. She did not say a word, she just listened and only shared her name that night. She was amazed at the struggles these ladies had been through. Then someone shared a testimony about her healing from the abuse. Bianca was astonished at what she had heard. So much of it was the same as her story. She began another weekly group meeting to receive healing. Is this what was wrong with her all this time? Could her guilt and hate be misplaced? She was now determined to find out. Chastain went to the group with her for support and to try to work through her eating disorder that had consumed her as a teenager. Her eating disorder paralleled Bianca's drinking. Midway through the group therapy, Bianca began realizing she was her own problem. By drinking and continuing to take the valium to escape the pain was only allowing what had happened to continue to hurt her. In the end, she was ready to write her testimony as well. But, there was

PART VII - Bianca

still Tucker. Other ladies had gone ahead and told their husbands, and their marriages were forever changed. Bianca was not sure she was that strong yet.

Tucker had noticed a definite change in Bianca. She had even gotten him to go to church with her. He did not know what it was that had changed in her but knew he wanted some of the peace she had received. Of course, he thought it might help their marriage.

Months later, Bianca was ready to give her testimony. She still had not told Tucker any of this sordid story. She asked him to come with her one night because she was going to share. She told him that he would hear things he had no idea about, and she did not want him to be mad, but this was the only way she could do it. She needed the support of the other ladies surrounding her or else he would never know the true her. Tucker did go with her. He had no words, only tears, as he listened intently to his wife's story. She felt as though a weight had been lifted but also wondered if her marriage was over. She could not blame him if it was. After going home, they stayed up and talked all night. They both took off work the next day just to be together. Now she agreed to the marriage counseling, and God was moving mightily in both of their lives and within their marriage. That is not to say they did not still have difficulties as everyone does. However, their marriage became stronger than it had ever been, and there were now new ways to cope with the stress of life

PART VII - Bianca

PART VII
SYBIL

PART VII - Sybil

Nausea was beginning to take over Sybil. The sickening memories, the way her parents would probably react, having a sheriff on hand was all taking a toll on her. Most of all, she did not want anything to happen to Jesse. First, they went to the sheriff's office to get someone to go with them. They already knew what to expect. Apparently, Gerard had contacted them to let them know what was happening. He had a friend that worked there.

Away they went, following the sheriff's car. When they arrived, the sheriff along with Gerard and Jesse went to the door. James couldn't believe this kid came back with the sheriff. Was he never going to get it? James was quite surprised to hear Jesse saying he and Sybil had gotten married that day. James immediately began to raise his voice, telling Jesse he had no right. The sheriff stepped in telling James, Jesse did have the right, and they were there to get Sybil's clothes and belongings. Jesse strolled out to the car and got Sybil. He walked her to the door, and James refused to let him in. He said he was agreeable to that as long as the sheriff was inside with her. Gerard then mentioned he had a legal advisor with him if they needed him as well. James realized he had been beaten. Rage was running through his body at Jesse. Who did that boy think he was? Then James looked at Sybil and retorted, you were used goods anyway. Get your stuff and get out. You will never step foot in this house again.

Sybil had already packed a lot of her things wanting to make this visit as short as possible. It was easy to see how mad James was, and as he turned on Jesse, Gerard shook his head and motioned toward the car. His legal advisor promptly came up and asked James if he had something he would like to say or do. They could see James's knuckles were white as he kept making them into a fist. Athena pleaded with Sybil to make this right with her dad so they could at least keep in touch. Sybil laughed out loud, asking do you really think I would ever want to see either of you again? You are more of a fool than I had thought. You deserve to live here with only dad keeping your head buried in the sand the same you have done through all of the abuse. It took Sybil a few trips, but she got everything she needed. If she had forgotten something, then that was just too bad.

As she walked back to the car, she hoped Jesse nor Gerard heard her statements to her mother. She didn't necessarily care that they

PART VII - Sybil

could hear her, but she had used the word abuse. She didn't want to lose Jesse. For now, she would just try not to think about it.

Once they left, Gerard announced she would need to hurry and repack because she had a plane to catch! She had no idea where they were going. Gerard laughed and reassured her that only she and Jesse were going. He sent them on a 6 night stay in Puerto Vallarta for an all-inclusive honeymoon! There was no end to the surprises of this day.

After a week of bliss, they happy couple returned. Jesse told her there was a lot about him she needed to know. Sybil had been concerned about his boss. Jesse's father had gotten him the job. He explained that his family owned a large medical supply facility and he had to prove he could be responsible, hold a job, not drink, and be a productive member of society before his dad would let him come back to work with him. Sybil would never have to work. Sybil was shocked but wanted to be a school teacher or counselor to help children like her. It was almost too much to take in. Jesse assured her she could do whatever her heart desired.

A few weeks later, Sybil saw her father downtown. He just glared at her at first. Then he had a lot to say. All negative and calling her horrible names. He told her just to wait. She would want to come crawling back home from that loser, and she would not have anywhere to go. He kept saying he would get her for this. When she least expected it, he would make her pay for what she had put them through. Eventually, he shut up and left. A small crowd had gathered. A gentleman asked if she needed assistance or for him to call the police. She quietly said no, ran her errands, and went home.

She needed treatment, therapy, or just anything that could help her. How could she explain all of this to Jesse without eventually telling him the truth? He had given her ample opportunity to have done so, but she just could not do it. She knew she needed to confide in him. How would he take it? Would he have their marriage annulled? She would completely lose it without him.

She began looking up marriage counselors. That was the only thing that could possibly help. She made an appointment. This was the hardest thing she had ever had to do. She may go insane if she did not.

At her first appointment, she was a total mess. As expected, the therapist thought her

PART VII - Sybil

husband should join them, and then she would not have to go through all of this twice, and the therapist would be there to mediate.

When Jesse got home, Sybil was a mess. She could not stop crying, and he could not understand half of what she said. Once she calmed down a bit, she was able to tell him about going to a marriage counselor. Jesse was very confused. He thought they were happy and expressed so. She tried to assure him that it was not about him; it was all her, but she needed him by her side as she got rid of the pain and memories that were going to destroy her. Jesse instantly recognized that this was what had caused the cutting in the first place. She just could not share it until they were at the therapist's office. She did not get one wink of sleep that night. The therapist had recognized her desperation and had moved some appointments around to make time for Sybil the very next day. They had an appointment at 10am.

Jesse felt so horrible. Sybil was distraught, and he had never seen her like this. Not even in the hospital. He had the same fear she did. What if she wanted to end their marriage? Was she wanting an annulment? When it came time to leave, Sybil was crying and shaking and really scaring Jesse. Once they arrived, they were ushered right in. The therapist already thought she knew what Sybil needed to share. She had seen it before, and she was prepared. The therapist had Sybil tell Jesse what had happened with her dad and then to share whatever was so heavily weighing her down. Sybil got up and got the whole box of tissues off the table and brought them back with her. She was not able to fully get out what had happened the day before. Jesse was unsure of some of the things her dad had said but was very concerned what all of this had to do with. She finally began to share her story of her childhood through a barrage of tears. Jesse began to cry that anyone could ever even think of hurting Sybil this way. He knew there was much more to this story, but he had the basics of it. Childhood sexual abuse and a mother that knew and did nothing. He pleaded with Sybil to let him sit near her and hold her. The therapist was so relieved to see his reaction. These types of situations usually did not have positive outcomes, and a several had ended in divorce.

Sybil could not look Jesse in the eye. She was so ashamed. He whispered it was not her fault and they would do whatever they needed

PART VII - Sybil

to in order to get her through this. The therapist then mentioned a women's group and had a pamphlet about it. She believed it would help. The ladies that ran it had been sexually abused as children also and worked to walk other women through it. Sybil agreed, and Jesse was so relieved. He was scared she would refuse. He could not stand seeing Sybil like this. Then he murmured and asked if this was why the cutting. He knew the answer, he needed to hear Sybil say it. As she said yes, she begged him to forgive her for not being honest, to begin with. The fact she had never told him broke his heart.

They left with the promise of going to the women's group and made an appointment with the therapist for next week.

At her first meeting, she discovered the ladies leading it were all Christians. She was not sure how she felt about that. They actually addressed that very subject when telling the group about themselves. They also had blamed God. Sybil could not believe what she was hearing. Of course, they invited the women in the group to church on Sunday. Sybil told Jesse all about it when she got home. He asked if she would like to go to church and learn some of the things the ladies were talking about. She had to admit she had mixed emotions, but she wanted whatever it was they had that they could be a peace with their pasts.

They began going to church together. They both wound up giving their lives to Christ. There was still a lot of work Sybil needed to do, but she was taking the right steps in the right direction. She knew she would spend the rest of her life looking over her shoulder for her dad and his wrath, but with God and Jesse, she knew she could handle it. She had a completely new lease on life, and it felt wonderful!!

Sybil invited Samantha over and told her the whole sordid story of her parents, Jesse, the wedding, getting her things and the honeymoon. Samantha was over the moon at the tale.

Jesse and Sybil invited Samantha and Allen to church with them. Sybil told Samantha about the group she was attending. Samantha burst into tears. As the tears dripped down her face, she managed to tell Sybil she had also been sexually abused since the fourth grade. They could not believe they both felt so awful they could not trust each other. Samantha started attending the group with Sybil. She also gave her life to Christ. At first, she had tremendous difficulty with forgiveness and understanding it

PART VII - Sybil

was for her, not her abuser. It took a long time to work through it all, but she allowed Christ to be her peace as she walked it out. It seemed more comfortable that her best friend had walked through it as well.

PART VII
CHASTAIN

PART VII - CHASTAIN

Rhett went to jail. He received the maximum sentence in Albuquerque of 9 years. Chastain was beside herself with excitement. She continued with therapy. She knew it was helping her but still had no self-worth and couldn't see value in herself. Donna continued her bible study. She and Robert were working on their relationship and were going to marriage counseling.

It took over a year for Donna to let Robert move back in. She had so much to work through herself. She needed to be confident she could forgive him and move forward. That simply took time.

Chastain became a part of the Chess Club. She was so thrilled! She quickly showed she was an opponent not to be taken for granted.

When she graduated, she had a scholarship for college. She was delighted! She had been taking her college basics already. She wanted to become a CPA. Her life had changed so dramatically since the days of her uncle living with them. Her dad was back home. They were choosing to live life to the fullest. Yes, he was still very busy with work but ensured he made time for her and her mom. They had gone on some spectacular vacations!! She had loved going skiing, and the Caribbean but her favorite had been traveling Europe. Memories and experiences she would always hold dear. Her mom was happier than Chastain ever recalled seeing her. It was almost embarrassing the way her mom and dad flirted with one another. Flowers came pretty regularly for her mom, and sometimes there was a bouquet for her as well. Despite all they had been through, they had definitely come out on top. They were all attending church together, and her father had become a deacon. Life was everything she could wish for. Now, on to the next chapters!

    When Chastain started college, her parents had helped her get an apartment. As long as her grades were good, they would take care of all the bills. Along the way, boys had paid attention to her, even asked her out, but she just could not do it. She hung out with them as friends. The thought of a relationship always brought back memories of Rhett. She kept praying that would pass one day. Rhett was rarely brought up in their home. When he was, Robert would start to rant. Then he usually stopped and quoted Proverbs 29:11 A fool gives full vent to his spirit, but a wise man quietly holds it back. He would tell her and her mom, he wanted to

PART VII - CHASTAIN

be a wise man, and the rant was over. He did not really give vent to the rant. He would get it stopped before it really got started.

After Chastain graduated from college, passed her exam, and went to work with another CPA. She now paid her own bills, and she was loving it. The years seem to pass so quickly. Before she knew it, her biggest fear had come true. Her uncle had been let out of prison. She had no idea where he was and still had a little fear of him. Her dad told her Rhett had moved away to get a new start. People here that knew him would never let him live down what he had done. Her apartment had an alarm system, so that gave her a much-needed feel of security.

Walking home after a late night at work seems like just the thing she needs. Tax season completely drains her, and she loves the cool night air. Stopping off for a cup of coffee to ward off the chill of the night, she just needs to clear her mind of numbers and clients. Working as a CPA is very rewarding even during the stress of this season. Busy streets in the distance remind her another long day has been wrapped up and the end of tax season is near. This makes her feel light and airy, knowing there's an end to the chaos.

Laura Schonlau

As she nears her apartment, the thought of a long hot bath with a glass of wine sounds fabulous. Being lost in her own thoughts, she doesn't pay much attention to her surroundings. That bath is sounding better and better the closer to home she gets. The dark shadows of the night engulfing her and would leave plenty of room for her thoughts to run wild if she allowed them to go there.

Stepping up to the porch of her apartment, she fumbles for keys in her purse. She shut the alarm off, but the darn porch light was out, leaving little visibility to find her keys. Finally, there they were. Buried into a deep pocket on the inside of her purse. She lets out a sigh of relief as she begins to unlock the door. Then she hears the footsteps that are coming near to her. Trying to hurry to get in, as a leery feeling takes over the pit of her stomach, he says her name. She looks back, but he has a dark hoody on, and she is frightened as she steps through the door. Before she can get it locked back, the figure shoves his way into her apartment. He has a large knife pointing at her. He threatens to gut her like a fish if she makes a sound. Then he lunges toward her, knocking her to the ground. In a flash, he had a piece of duct tape over her

PART VII - CHASTAIN

mouth and began dragging her to the bedroom. As she's struggling to get out of his grip, the candlesticks on the coffee table tumble over, the small table in the hallway gets knocked onto its side, the knife cuts her forearm, and he throws her onto the bed. Stricken with fear, she doesn't know what to do or how to protect herself in this position. Visions of her childhood begin flashing through her mind, and she knows, deep inside, no man will ever take advantage of her again. As he comes toward her and lifts the hem of her skirt, he tells her, "once I told you one day I would own you, but you thought you had escaped". She begins to come to her senses. He's overpowering her when suddenly she grabs the ice pick she keeps under the pillow for protection in case anyone ever did get this close to her. Without a moment's hesitation, she stabs him in the neck. A deep animal groan came from him. She shoved him, and he rolled over on the bed. She jumped up, realizing she still had the tape over mouth and ripped it off. There was a pool of blood forming on her bed from the man. She ran for her purse to get her cell phone to call 911.

When the police arrived, she was ushered out of the apartment. Her neighbors had come out to see what was going on, and it was then reality sunk in, and she began to sob. What was a horrible situation just got worse when she found out her attacker was. Rhett. It was Uncle Rhett. Never again would she have to worry for one moment about him.

    No charges were filed against her as it was obviously self-defense and her security cameras had caught it all. Now, maybe she would have a full chance at life. She stayed with her parents for a couple of weeks. When all was said and done, she returned home full of hope for the future. She began seeing her therapist again with the hopes of actually being able to have a relationship and possibly get married one day. Whatever he did for a career was unimportant. She needed a God fearing man, that would put God first then her. One that would pray over her, and they could walk out a marriage full of God's love and grace.

PART VII - CHASTAIN

Epilogue

Epilogue

Bottom line: if you had a bad father growing up, it's hard to imagine a good father. I struggled with that for years as well. Know this: God is a Good Good Father.

I know God wants to see your healing. To see you happy. So do I. So does your family. My beliefs don't have to be yours. You can worship who/ whatever you want. All I want is to see/ know you've been set free.

If you're struggling, I want to offer you a group you can join. In this group, you are not alone. You'll hear about other women who experienced the same things you have. Stories of hope and happiness. ABR **https://www.facebook.com/groups/585261405323807/** - Abused & Beautifully Redeemed.

You NEED to know you're loved, lovable and you're not hopeless, helpless or the many other negative thoughts you have.

Please feel free to send a personal message if you're not ready to be in the discussion yet.

Meet
Laura Schonlau

Laura Schonlau

Born in Oklahoma, Laura has a huge heart for broken/hurting women. Being abused as a child gives her an ability to relate to them by hearing more than just their words. She hears their hearts and the underlying hurt. She has endured all of the emotions they go through; pain, hate, low self-esteem, unforgiveness, and the tears. The many, many tears she has shed, just like them, and for them. She has spent the last eighteen years helping women help themselves, move to places of forgiveness, and build self-esteem.

This book was published by

First Time
Press

10% of all the revenue from this book goes to support missions work. We hope you enjoyed this author's self-edited work.

First Time Press exists to give promising authors a platform to publish their early works. Since its founding, First Time Press has eagerly sought out and received submissions from authors worldwide looking for a chance to be noticed for their extraordinary work.

Each year, First Time Press receives self-submitted manuscripts from undiscovered authors looking to use their talents to bring God glory. Each work is reviewed and examined by an award-winning team of creators. Five manuscripts are hand-picked each year for their raw excellence (ranging anywhere from sci-fi to biographies). These manuscripts are then edited by the author and published "as is" to showcase the creator's undiscovered talent.

First Time Press looks to encourage and celebrate the achievements of those who have a passion and a calling to write. All publishing expenses are covered, and there is no out of pocket cost for these authors once chosen for publication. 80% of all revenue generated from the sales of First Time Press books is given back to their respective authors. Only 20% is deducted, 10% to cover the cost of operations and 10% donated to a missions work.

Other titles from

FIRST TIME
PRESS

OTHER TITLES FROM

Other Worlds and their stories
By J. Riley Peak

The question regarding whether or not other planets share earth's unique ability to rear life is a question many ask. However, I resign myself to the idea that I must leave such a search alone, for why bother talking about planets when one can speak about worlds?

Hearts at War
By Rob Winblad

Sergeant Rick Newman has shipped to Afghanistan with the Marines. After a mission goes wrong and his fiancee's brother is killed in action, he blames himself for her brother's death and the subsequent dissolution of their relationship. Running from the demons that haunt him, he must find it in his heart to forgive himself, even as she has forgiven him.

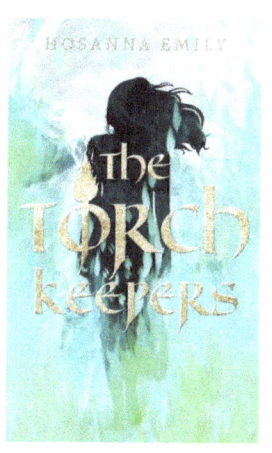

The Torch Keepers
By Hosanna Emily

A revolution sweeps across the kingdom of Érkeos. A girl finds her city engulfed in the Liberation's emerald flames. But, when she meets Rekém, she rebels against the King. Now Kadira and Rekém could bring destruction to the entire kingdom.

www.ingramcontent.com/pod-product-compliance
Lightning Source LLC
Chambersburg PA
CBHW072149100526
44589CB00015B/2157